★Units of
Instruction
for gifted learners

Units of Instruction

for gifted learners

by diana brigham, jessica fell,
constance simons, kathy strunk,
& anthony yodice

Routledge
Taylor & Francis Group

NEW YORK AND LONDON

First published in 2006 by Prufrock.Press Inc.

Published in 2021 by Routledge
605 Third Avenue, New York, NY 10017
2 Park Square, Milton Park, Abingdon, Oxon OX14 4RN

Routledge is an imprint of the Taylor & Francis Group, an informa business.

© 2006 by Taylor & Francis Group

Illustrations by Mike Eustis

ISBN: 9781032142821 (hbk)
ISBN: 9781593631963 (pbk)

DOI: 10.4324/9781003239369

Contents

Crossing the Land to Freedom
–Developed by Kathy Strunk

Unit Overview: This is an interdisciplinary unit that uses literature and reading activities to teach students about how slaves lived and found freedom. Students will complete a Web quest in which they learn about the Underground Railroad, activists and abolitionists, and research laws and people that contributed to the abolition of slavery. Students will write and present reports from their research. Students will consider the wants and needs of slaves when they made their journey to freedom.

Resources Needed:
- Multiple copies of the book *Sweet Clara and the Freedom Quilt* by Debra Hopkinson, 1995, ISBN# 0-67987-472-0
- paper
- U.S. map
- pens/pencils
- computers with Internet access
- encyclopedia/reference books
- the book *Follow the Drinking Gourd* by Jeanette Winter, 1999, ISBN# 0-83358-047-7
- overhead projector/smartboard
- colored construction paper
- markers
- camera

Helpful Resources:
- *Aunt Harriet's Underground Railroad in the Sky* by Faith Ringgold, 1999, ISBN# 0-78578-483-7
- *The Story of Ruby Bridges* by Robert Coles, 1995, ISBN# 0-59057-281-4
- *Frederick Douglass Fights For Freedom* by Margaret Davidson, 1988, ISBN# 0-59042-218-9
- *The Quilt-Block History of Pioneer Days* by Mary Cobb, 1995, ISBN# 1-56294-692-7

- *Portraits of African-American Heroes* by Tonya Bolden, 2003, ISBN# 0-52457-043-3
- http://www.gale.com/free_resources/index.htm
- http://www2.lhric.org/pocantico/tubman/gourd.htm

Lesson 1

Grade Level: 3–5

Approximate Length of Time: 1–2 hours

Prerequisite Knowledge:

- slavery
- making predictions about a story
- using contextual clues to identify new vocabulary words

Rationale: Through studying literature and discussion, students will learn how the institution of slavery affected the personal lives of African Americans, as well as other ethnic groups worldwide. Rereading for contextual vocabulary words will further develop comprehension of the text.

National Standards Addressed:

- Identify reasons people formed communities and describe how individuals, events, and ideas have shaped communities over time.
- Compare ways people in communities meet their needs in the past and present.
- Use geographic tools to collect, analyze, and interpret data.
- Identify examples of organizations that serve the common good.
- Identify the contributions of people of various racial, ethnic, and religious groups to the United States.
- Listen to solve problems, gather information, or appreciate stories.
- Read for enjoyment, to solve problems, to gather information, and to extend vocabulary.
- Write to record ideas and reflections for a variety of audiences.

Objectives: Students will be able to:

- in pairs, explain the meaning of vocabulary words by using context clues in a story; and
- individually compare his or her feelings to Clara and Jack's and explain what freedom means to him or her in three paragraphs.

Materials:

- multiple copies of the book *Sweet Clara and the Freedom Quilt* by Debra Hopkinson
- Book Bits
- U.S. map
- Vocabulary List worksheet
- paper, pen, or pencil

Procedure:

Opening Review: In a class discussion, talk about making predictions about a story and how to use contextual clues to discover the meaning of vocabulary words. The teacher will model these procedures by writing the following sentence on the board: *The seamstress will need material, needles, and thread to sew my new dress.* The teacher will show how the word *sew* tells what the seamstress does and the words *material*, *needles*, and *thread* show what the seamstress uses. This sentence also tells the reader that the story might be about a seamstress.

Motivation or Introductory Approach: "Today, we are going to read about a special group of people, but before we do, will all the students with blonde hair go to the back of the room and all the other students come to the front. I want all of the students in the back of the room to bring a sharpened pencil to a student in the front of the room. The students in the front of the room can be seated. (Allow time for the students to sit down.) Students in the back of the room can now sit down."

Development of Lesson:

1. The teacher will pass around the envelope of Book Bits and have each student reach inside and remove one slip of paper. Have each student read the quote on the slip of paper to themselves. After reading the quote, students should take out a scrap piece of paper and write what they think the story will be about. After 2 minutes, have each student read their quote and then share his or her story prediction with the class.

2. Show the book *Sweet Clara and the Freedom Quilt* to the class, and read the name of the book and the author. Tell students that they should think about the following questions as you are reading the book to them:
   - Was Clara given a choice about working? Why?
   - Would you prefer to work inside or outside? Why?

3. Begin being reading the story. After reading through page 4 of the text, ask for responses to the questions.
   Tell students to think about these questions as you read the next two pages:
   - What was the Underground Railroad?
   - Who was involved in the Underground Railroad?

4. Have a student point out the Ohio River and Canada on the map and estimate the distance between the regions. Tell students to think about this distance, as well as the following question as you read the next three pages to them.
   - What does Clara say about dreaming?
   - Listen for clues that tell where Clara and Jack are going.

5. Tell students to think about the following question as you finish reading the story.
   - What kind of supplies would Clara and Jack need for their journey?

Closure: Have students return to their original seats. Ask students why they think you separated them as you did. Explain that you grouped them according to a common characteristic they shared with the rest of their group (i.e., hair color) and that is how people were grouped during the time period in the book—according to race.

Assessment:

Formative—Have a class discussion using the following questions:

- How did people become slaves? Is the practice of owning another person fair?
- How could you use landmarks to create a map in another way?
- How did the practice of slavery cause conflict between the northern and southern states?
- If the slaves had worked for wages would they still have wanted to be free?
- What reasons did the southern states have to own slaves?
- Were Clara and Jack the only slaves that escaped?

Summative—Students will compare their feelings about being grouped to those of Clara and Jack in a paragraph. A scoring guide will be used as a guideline for the student and as a way to assess his or her writing.

Independent Activities/Lesson Extension/Adaptations:

- Group students in pairs and give each group a list of vocabulary words with page numbers and a copy of *Sweet Clara and the Freedom Quilt*. Explain to the pairs of students that they are a "Mystery Group." One student will be the detective and find the clues in the section of text that leads to the meaning of the vocabulary word. The other student will be the reporter and write the clues next to the vocabulary word.
- Have students describe in a paragraph how they felt when they were placed in a group because of a common characteristic, and in another paragraph compare their feelings to those of Clara and Jack when they were grouped because of their race.

lesson 1
book bits for sweet clara and the freedom quilt

(Teachers: Copy this sheet and cut each Book Bits strip for the activity in Lesson 1)

We went north, following the trail of the freedom quilt. Mostly we hid during the day and walked at night.

Me and Jack left Home Plantation in a dark thunderstorm.

She touched the stitches lightly, her fingers moving slowly over the last piece I'd added—a hidden boat that would carry us across the Ohio River.

"That swamp next to Home Plantation is a nasty place. But listen up, Clara, and I'll tell you how I thread my way in and out of there as smooth as yo' needle in that cloth."

Sometimes I had to wait to get the right kind of cloth—I had blue calico and flowered blue silk for creeks and rivers, and greens and blue-greens for the fields, and white sheeting for roads.

I drew a little square for Big House, a line of boxes for the cabins of the Quarters, and some bigger squares for the fields east of Big House. I drew as much as I'd pieced together.

I saw the paterollers and I knew someone had run away.

Aunt Rachel say, "Sweet Clara, what kind of pattern you makin' in that quilt? Aine no pattern I ever seen." Then I started piecin' the scraps of cloth with the scraps of things I was learnin'.

And how could I make a map that wouldn't be washed away by the rain—a map that would show the way to freedom?

I took a stick and started making a picture in the dirt of all I could see. But how could I make a picture of things far away that I couldn't see?

---

lesson 1
book bits for sweet clara and the freedom quilt, continued

"You run away and get caught, you be beaten."

One of the men replied in a quiet voice, "It be easy if you could get a map."

"The Railroad will get you all the way to Canada. Then you free forever."

"Once you get that far, the Underground Railroad will carry you across."

"There been too many runaways last summer," one of the drivers said.

I was hearing about all kinds of new places and things.

One day two white men come to see the master.

So I changed from a field hand to a seamstress.

lesson 1
vocabulary list for sweet clara and the freedom quilt

Mystery Group Members _____

Directions: Read the section of the story on the page number listed in the second column. Identify clues that lead to the meaning of the vocabulary words, and write them in the third column under "Clues."

Vocabulary Word	Page	Clues
seamstress	3	
overseer	5	
contrary	7	
paterollers	10	
squirrel	16	
quarters	16	
buzzing	17	

lesson 1
writing assignment for sweet clara and the freedom quilt

Directions: In the space below, compare your feelings about being grouped in class to the way Clara and Jack must have felt when they were grouped because of their skin color.
Suggested length: 2 paragraphs.

_____

_____

_____

_____

_____

_____

_____

_____

_____

_____

_____

_____

_____

_____

lesson 1
writing evaluation

Writing assignment: Comparison paper for *Sweet Clara and the Freedom Quilt*

Points available	Criteria	Points Earned
5	Writes 2 or more paragraphs. Sentences are complete. Handwriting is neat, legible, and error free. Followed punctuation and capitalization rules.	
4	Writes 2 paragraphs. Sentences are complete. Handwriting is neat and legible, but contains errors. Followed punctuation and capitalization rules.	
3	Writes less than 2 paragraphs. Sentences are incomplete. Handwriting is legible, but not neat and error free. Followed punctuation and capitalization rules.	
2	Writes less than 2 paragraphs. Sentences are incomplete. Handwriting is messy, contains errors. Did not follow punctuation and capitalization rules.	
1	Did not complete assignment.	

Total _____/5

Comments:_____

_____

_____

_____

_____

_____

Lesson 2

Grade Level: 3–5

Approximate Length of Time: 1–2 hours

Prerequisite Knowledge:

- Underground Railroad
- significant African Americans, laws, and states associated with slavery
- how to navigate the Internet
- preparing an outline

Rationale: Students will learn how to navigate the Internet to research events, places, and people who have impacted the society in which they live.

National Standards Addressed:

- Identify important social changes of the 19th century, including the Industrial Revolution, westward expansion, and the Civil War.
- Describe important issues, events, and individuals of the 20th century.
- Describe political, economic, and physical regions in the United States.
- Describe the characteristics and benefits of the free enterprise system in the United States.
- Summarize fundamental rights of American citizens.
- Identify the contributions of people of various racial, ethnic, and religious groups to the United States.
- Identify important ideas in the Declaration of Independence and the U.S. Constitution.
- Generate relevant research using multiple sources of information.
- Compose, organize, and revise letters, essays, records, and research papers.

Objectives: Students will be able to:

- in groups of four, explore the process of the Underground Railroad using the Internet; and
- individually, prepare a report on a significant African American, law, or state associated with slavery and present the report as part of a group.

Materials:

- computers with Internet access
- encyclopedias and other reference books
- report criteria worksheets
- note-taking outline
- peer/self evaluation rubric

Procedure:

Opening Review: "Yesterday, we talked about the practice of owning another person and whether this was a fair practice or not." Ask the students to discuss the following questions:

- In the story we read yesterday, what was Clara's job on the plantation?
- Explain the importance of the quilt that Clara made. What did the quilt represent?
- Would you have helped someone escape? How?
- If you lived in a northern state, how could you help the people in the south?
- At one time, it was not against the law to own another person. Was this a fair law? Why or why not?

Review the following vocabulary:

- *conscience*—the feeling one has to do right or be good
- *abolitionist*—a person who wants to end the practice of slavery and its effect on society
- *activist*—someone who takes direct action against the practice of slavery

Motivation or Introductory Approach: "Today, we are going to take a trip with a person who was largely responsible for organizing the Underground Railroad. Her name was Harriet Tubman. As a class, we will do webbing for the vocabulary words."
Development of Lesson:
1. Have the students think about the questions below as they take their journey. It is helpful to have questions on the board or overhead for the students to see.
2. Place students in groups of 3–5, depending on the number of available computers.
3. Have them go to National Geographic's *The Underground Railroad* Web site at http://www.nationalgeographic.com/features/99/railroad and enjoy their journey. Here are the questions your students should answer:
   - What is the difference between an activist and an abolitionist?
   - What was the role of the abolitionist?
   - What was the role of the activist?
   - If no one knew where Canada was, how could you find out?

Closure: "We now know more about slavery and how slaves found their way to freedom." Have students respond to the above questions.

Assessment:

Formative—The teacher will observe the students while they are doing research on the Internet and by any other means to see if they are taking notes on their given subject.
Summative—Students will write and give an oral report on their research subject according to scoring guide. They will have a peer and self-evaluation of their oral report.

Independent Activities/Lesson Extension/Adaptations:

Place students in groups of three. In each group one student will research a person, one student will research a law, and one student will research a state that had a role during the time of slavery. The students will choose a topic or person from the list provided to each group and write a report on their topic or person according to given criteria.

lesson 2
research topics for
group reports

Significant people: http://www.famousamericans.net
- Harriet Tubman
- Sojourner Truth
- Thomas Garrett
- William Still
- Frederick Douglass
- Susan B. Anthony

States/places: http://www.50states.com
- Maryland
- Delaware
- Pennsylvania
- New York
- Georgia
- Kentucky

Laws relevant to slavery: http://www.ourdocuments.gov/content.php?page=milestone
- Emancipation Proclamation (1863)
- 13th Amendment to the U.S. Constitution
- 14th Amendment to the U.S. Constitution
- 15th Amendment to the U.S. constitution
- Fugitive Slave Act of 1793—http://www.u-s-history.com/pages/h480.html
- Fugitive Slave Act of 1850—http://www.u-s-history.com/pages/h137.html

lesson 2
group reports

Directions: Research your chosen topic. Write a report on your topic that includes the information below. This outline will also be used during group presentations for taking notes.

Report outline for significant people:
1. What is the name of the person you are studying?
2. What is his or her date and place of birth?
3. What was his or her role at birth? Was he or she a slave or a free citizen?
4. What other roles did this person assume during his or her life?
5. What are some significant contributions he or she made to society?

Report outline for significant place:
1. What is the name and capital of this state?
2. Name all of the states or bodies of water that surround this state.
3. When did it get its statehood?
4. Was this state for or against owning slaves?
5. What was the significance of the state during this time period?

Report outline for laws:
1. What is the name of the law or act you are studying?
2. When was the law passed?
3. Who passed the law?
4. Who did the law affect?
5. What was the significance of the law?

Lesson 3

Grade Level: 3–5

Approximate Length of Time: 1–2 hours

Prerequisite Knowledge:

- taking notes
- U.S. Constitution

Rationale: Students will learn from each other as they read and listen to reports while taking notes. They will connect events in history to understand our society today by looking at the way state laws and people have changed over time.

National Standards Addressed:

- Identify important social changes of the 19th century, including the Industrial Revolution, westward expansion, and the Civil War.
- Describe important issues, events, and individuals of the 20th century.
- Describe political, economic, and physical regions in the United States.
- Describe the characteristics and benefits of the free enterprise system in the United States.
- Summarize fundamental rights of American citizens.
- Identify the contributions of people of various racial, ethnic, and religious groups to the United States.
- Identify important ideas in the Declaration of Independence and the U.S. Constitution.
- Generate relevant research using multiple sources of information.
- Compose, organize, and revise letters, essays, records, and research papers.

Objectives: Students will be able to:

- in groups of three, develop a written report from an outline;
- as individual members of a group, orally give a report; and
- complete a self-evaluation and peer evaluation after completion of reports.

Materials:

- computer with Internet access
- list of Web sites
- encyclopedias and other reference books
- maps
- report outline
- report topics

Procedure:

Opening Review: "This week we have talked about events, places, and people that played significant roles during the time of slavery. These affected the society that we live in today in a number of ways." Generate responses from students on ways they feel our society has been affected. Ask the following questions of your students:

- How did the acquisition and ownership of slaves lead to the creation of laws in the United States?
- What benefit are these laws to us today?

Motivation or Introductory Approach: "Today, you will work in your groups to finish your reports that you began yesterday."
Development of Lesson:
1. Have students get in their groups from yesterday to finish their reports. Circulate among the groups to offer advice or help as needed. Set the timer for 45 minutes.
2. The groups will present their reports. Each student will get a peer evaluation for each group.
3. Ask each group the following questions after they have completed their reports:
   - What sources did you use to find information on your topic?
   - Was it easier to work within a group as compared to working by yourself?
   - What is something you learned about your topic that you didn't know before doing research?

Closure: "We have heard about significant people, places, and events that helped to shape the United States as we know it today." Ask the following questions:

- What does an activist do? Can you give me the name of an activist and tell why that person is significant?
- What is an abolitionist? Can you give the name of one and discuss why that person is significant?
- Why was freedom so important to people like Clara and Jack?
- What is one way that escaped slaves became free?

Assessment:

Formative—The teacher will observe the students while they are working on and giving oral reports.
Summative—The students will do a peer evaluation on each group's presentation and a self-evaluation on their participation in the group. The teacher will grade the written report according to the scoring guide.

Independent Activities/Lesson Extension/Adaptations:

1. Complete peer/self-evaluations and turn in reports and evaluations.
2. Give each student a copy of the song and translation from *Follow the Drinking Gourd* to take home and read. Tell them they may practice playing the song on their recorder, if they have one.
3. Collaborate with the music teacher to tape the music and have a choral singing. The music teacher may also have students play the song in music class on their recorders, if they have them.

Name_____ **lesson 3** Date_____

student self-evaluation

Directions: Put a check mark in the column that best describes your participation in your group.

	Yes	Sometimes	No
I asked questions when there was something I didn't understand.			
I helped the people in my group.			
I did my best work.			
I worked quietly and stayed on task.			
My part of the presentation was complete.			

Date_____

lesson 3
peer evaluation

Directions: Circle the number that best describes the presentation of the group, with 1 denoting the least effective and 3 being the most effective presentation.

Presentation was informative (Did you learn something?)	1	2	3
Presentation was interesting (Did it hold your attention?)	1	2	3
Presentation was clear (Could you hear and understand the speaker?)	1	2	3
Use of visual aids (Did they present maps, pictures?)	1	2	3
Did all group members participate in the presentation?	1	2	3

Total _____/15

Comments _____

_____

_____

Lesson 4

Grade Level: 3–5

Approximate Length of Time: 1–2 hours

Prerequisite Knowledge:

- wants and needs
- slavery

Rationale: Students will see how the northern states working with the southern states helped to give the oppressed people of the south a new way of life that consequently changed the status of different cultures as we see them today. Students will develop an understanding of music used in another culture for a predetermined reason by translating the textual messages of a song and performing the song.

National Standards Addressed:

- Compare ways people in communities meet their needs in the past and present.
- Use cardinal and intermediate directions, scale, compass rose, grid, and symbols to locate places and interpret maps and globes.
- Explain basic economic patterns of early societies in the United States.
- Explain the importance of individual participation in the democratic process.
- Retell the heroic deeds of real and fictional heroes who have helped shape the culture of communities.
- Listen to solve problems, gather information, or appreciate stories.
- Listen to identify the musical elements of literary language, such as rhymes, repeated sounds, or instances of onomatopoeia.
- Make and explain important inferences in a story.
- Write to record ideas and reflections for a variety of audiences.

Objectives: Students will be able to:

- as a group, sing and interpret hidden messages in a song; and
- individually, evaluate wants and needs in a written format.

Materials:

- *Follow the Drinking Gourd* by Jeanette Winter
- words and music notation from the book for each student
- overhead projector/smartboard
- scoring guide
- map

Procedure:

Opening Review: "When I say that African Americans were oppressed through slavery, what do I mean?" (Allow time for students to answer.) "Oppression means that someone else tells you what to do, when to do it, where to live, and so on. You don't have control of your actions; someone else does. Why did we see more oppression in the southern states than in the northern states?"

Motivation or Introductory Approach: "The music I sent home with you last night came from the book *Follow the Drinking Gourd.* We are going to read this story and interpret the meaning of the text to understand how the slaves used the hidden meanings to escape."

Development of Lesson:

1. Show students the book, and tell the name and author.
2. Read *Follow the Drinking Gourd.* The students will echo the teacher singing the song from the story. Then they will sing the song as a class. The class will interpret the hidden messages in the song and discuss how the messages were used to guide the slaves along the Underground Railroad.
3. The teacher will guide a discussion using the questions below:
   - What did the drinking gourd represent?
   - What was the significance of following the drinking gourd?
   - What phrase represents winter and spring?
   - What are quail?
   - Who is the old man and how does he help the slaves?
   - How did the slaves distinguish the Tombigbee River?
   - What body of water located in Tennessee did the slaves follow?
   - Which river joined the Tennessee River? (Call on students to locate the rivers on the map.)
4. Discuss the difference between wants and needs. Use examples such as food, clothing, shelter, toys, books, and so forth to guide the students in recognizing what people need to survive and what people just want. Have students provide examples and discuss how people could produce the items we need. Use a Semantic Feature Analysis on the board using examples (see example on p. 23).

Closure: "Today, we have explored another way that slaves found freedom—through hidden messages. The first way was through Clara's quilt and now through the words of a song. We have also learned how other people helped the slaves along the way. How did the people in the northern states cooperate with the people in the southern states to help the escaped slaves? How did this help to shape our society?"

Assessment:

Formative—The teacher will question the students while reading the story to evaluate their understanding.
Summative—The students will interpret passages of text for hidden meanings. Students will compare the wants and needs of newly freed slaves with their own wants and needs in a written format.

Independent Activities/Lesson Extension/Adaptations:

Students will explain how the slaves escaped and what they would need to take with them on their journey north. They will also evaluate and explain ways in which the slaves could provide for their needs when they reached Canada. This short essay will be evaluated with a scoring guide.

lesson 4
words to "follow the drinking gourd"

Follow the drinking gourd!
Follow the drinking gourd.
For the old man is awaiting for to carry you to freedom
If you follow the drinking gourd.

When the sun comes back and the first quail calls,
Follow the drinking gourd,
For the old man is awaiting for to carry you to freedom
If you follow the drinking gourd.

The riverbank makes a very good road,
The dead trees will show you the way,
Left foot, peg foot traveling on,
Following the drinking gourd.

The river ends between two hills,
Follow the drinking gourd,
There's another river on the other side,
Follow the drinking gourd.

Where the great big river meets the little river,
Follow the drinking gourd,
The old man is awaiting for to carry you to freedom
If you follow the drinking gourd.

lesson 4
example: semantic
feature analysis

Follow the Drinking Gourd

Complete on the board or overhead.

clothing	bread	love	food
house	shoes	television	sunshine
friends	books	cars	safety

Wants	Needs

lesson 4
writing rubric

Directions: In a short essay, explain slavery, how the slaves escaped, and what they would need to take with them on their journey north. Also, explain how the slaves could provide for their needs when they reached Canada. Use the rubric below as a guideline when writing your essay.
Suggested length: 1–2 pages

Organization of essay (70 points)

Points Available	Criteria	Points Earned
10	Essay has an original title	
10	Includes an explanation of a slave	
10	Explains how slaves escaped including the route taken	
10	Includes at least three or more states, rivers, and landmarks that slaves traveled through	
10	Includes at least five items the slaves would need to take on the journey	
10	Explains at least one way slaves could provide for their needs in Canada	
10	Includes at least one person or place that hid escaped slaves	

Grammar (30 points)

Points Available	Criteria	Points Earned
10	Punctuation rules followed	
10	Capitalization rules followed	
10	Words used correctly in complete sentences	

Total _____ /100

Lesson 5

Grade Level: 3–5

Approximate Length of Time: 1–2 hours

Prerequisite Knowledge:

- geometric shapes
- slavery
- freedom
- U.S. Constitution
- Underground Railroad
- significant African Americans

Rationale: By reviewing concepts, events, people, and places, students will develop an understanding of how past cultures and societies have affected our present society.

National Standards Addressed:

- Identify reasons people formed communities and describe how individuals, events, and ideas have shaped communities over time.
- Listen to solve problems, gather information, or appreciate stories.
- Write to record ideas and reflections for a variety of audiences.
- Write for varied purposes, including to achieve a sense of audience, make precise word choices, and create vivid images.
- Identify and extend patterns of ordered pairs.
- Identify congruent shapes.

Objectives:

- individually, make connections between slavery, freedom, and the Underground Railroad in a class discussion; and
- as a class, discuss and evaluate how laws shaped our society.

Materials:

- colored construction paper
- markers
- camera
- quilt grid game

Procedure:

Opening Review: Ask your students the following questions:

- How did the acquisition and ownership of slaves lead to the creation of laws in the United States?
- How do these laws benefit us today?
- What is an activist? What role would an activist assume in today's society?
- Why is freedom so important to us today?

- What laws or amendments guarantee individual rights?
- Is the practice of owning another person a fair practice? Why?

Motivation or Introductory Approach:
"Today, we are going to create a wall quilt that displays our ideas and feelings about historical events, people, and places. We will invite the principal and other classes to look at our quilt, so we must do our best work. But, before we begin, we are going to play a game on a quilt grid. The shapes you create on the grid will resemble a quilt that has been pieced together. Remember, in the story *Sweet Clara and the Freedom Quilt*, Clara pieced a quilt together to use as a map to freedom."

Development of Lesson:
1. Arrange students in pairs. Give each pair two different colored markers and a quilt grid. Explain the procedures of the game to the class. Review polygons and show examples. Set the timer for 15 minutes and circulate among the pairs to answer any questions. End the game and begin the wall quilt.
2. Give each student a sheet of construction paper and markers. The teacher will say a word or phrase such as *slavery, freedom, Underground Railroad, 14th Amendment,* and *Harriet Tubman.* The students will write or draw the first thing that comes into mind on their sheet of construction paper after the teacher says a word or phrase. Students may add pictures of significant people and states from their research to the wall quilt.
3. Place the completed sheets of construction paper on the wall to form a quilt. The principal and other classes will be invited to look at the wall quilt. Students may take turns explaining the words, symbols, and pictures.

Closure: "Today, we have explored our feelings and ideas about past events." Have students explain any incidences of discrimination.

Assessment:

Summative—Students will interpret questions and comments made by the teacher into individual ideas by creating a wall quilt with pictures, words, and symbols to represent their ideas of this time in history.

Independent Activities/Lesson Extension/Adaptations:

Students may design an invitation for the principal and other classes to view their wall quilt. Take each student's picture beside the quilt with him or her pointing to his or her contribution.

First player _____ Second player _____

Procedure
- First player colors in any single small triangle of the quilt grid.
- Second player colors in any other small triangle of the grid.
- Players then alternate turns coloring in small triangles anywhere on the grid.
- The game ends when the grid is completely colored.
- Points are awarded for the following shapes, each made up of four triangles:

Square: 1 point   Triangle: 2 points   Rectangle: 3 points   Parallelogram: 4 points

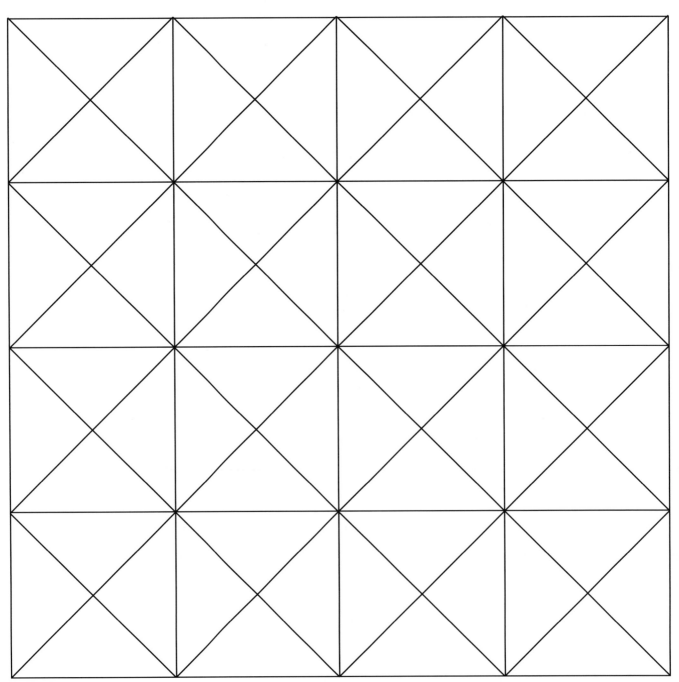

Media Blitz
–Developed by Anthony Yodice

Unit Overview: This is a social studies unit that may be used for any curriculum based on a region of the world, such as Europe, Africa, or Asia. It can be used for small or large groups, including an entire class. It allows students to be creative in their approach as to how they present their information. It also teaches the students research skills and reinforces writing and technology skills. The unit also allows classes to investigate how modern mass media affects the world and how each medium is structured and created, while covering content for the region being studied. All of this is accomplished while producing real-world products that may be shared with a variety of audiences.

Resources Needed:
- Internet access for student research
- A classroom subscription to a news-based periodical
- Tape (audio) recording and video recording hardware

Helpful Resources:
- Media and American Democracy from the Bill of Rights Institute. Available at http://www.BillofRightsInstitute.org.
- *USA Today*'s education Web site: http://www.usatoday.com/educate/home. htm

Lesson 1
Current Events

Grade Level: 5–8

Approximate Length of Time: Ongoing

Prerequisite Knowledge:

- sorting through and reading a newspaper
- summarizing information
- vocabulary: bibliography, periodical, bias, editorial, headline, byline

Rationale: This assignment familiarizes students with the mass media in America and with newspapers in particular. This will be important for the following projects.

National Standards Addressed: The content standards covered will depend on the content area for which the assignment is used and the stories the student chooses. The skills addressed are:

- The student applies critical-thinking skills to organize and use information acquired from a variety of sources, including electronic technology.
- The student communicates in written, oral, and visual forms.

Objectives: Students will be able to:

- use periodicals to gain information about the content areas being covered,
- summarize the article chosen,
- evaluate the actions of the participants in the story, and
- orally present their article and evaluation to the class.

Materials: A variety of periodicals (Web sites can be used only if they are from reputable news sources)

Procedure:

Opening: This lesson is a homework assignment that can be used repeatedly over any length of time—a quarter, semester, or year. It has students use many social studies skills and teaches a variety of content areas. Students look in newspapers and magazines for articles of interest and write about them according to the given format. Usually, students are restricted to stories from areas that are being studied at some point that year. Teachers may make the selection criteria more or less restrictive depending on their objectives. Newspapers should be available in class and the first current event assignment should be completed in class. The instructor should provide feedback so that there is improvement in the assignments as they continue throughout the unit.

Development of Lesson:

1. This activity should be assigned once a week for the duration of the unit. (It can also be used throughout the year with other units with little or no modification.)
2. Students should be given the Current Events worksheet and the rubric. Be sure to go over both with the class and answer any questions. Students need to be aware that the format is sequential and steps cannot be skipped.
3. Provide class time for students to locate and read their articles or assign the project for homework.
4. On the day the current events are due, students should be given a chance to share their articles with the class. Classmates should be allowed to ask questions about the articles shared.

Closure: Sharing the articles is a great way to wrap up the lesson. The teacher should use probing questions to get the students to connect the articles to what is being learned in class at the time. For example, an article about Prime Minister Tony Blair visiting the U.S. could be connected to a discussion of Great Britain's political systems, the state of the relationship between the two countries, or the role of a head of state.

Assessment: Students' articles will be assessed using the Current Events Rubric (see p. 35).

Independent Activities/Lesson Extension/Adaptations:

*   Ask students to follow their story in the newspaper for a few more days to see what develops.
*   Ask students to research the answers to any questions they or their classmates had about the article.
*   Purchase a classroom subscription to a periodical and give time in class to read articles of interest and to read articles as a class and discuss them.

lesson 1
current events worksheet

Keep this someplace safe. You will use it every week!

You can choose an article about any topic (except sports). Your article must be long enough to respond with a thoughtful summary and discussion. Newspaper articles can be up to 2 weeks old, and magazine articles can be up to 2 months old, if it is a monthly publication.

In each article review, you will need to address the following items:

- Bibliographical information
- Title of article
- Title of periodical (newspaper or magazine)
- Date of article
- Author
- Summary:
  - Who is the article about?
  - Where did the story take place?
  - What is the article about?
  - Why did this event happen or why is it newsworthy?
  - How did it happen?
- Reaction

Write a well thought out paragraph about this article. Possible topics to discuss include why you chose the article, why it is important, what you think the outcome will be or if you agree or disagree with the outcome, your opinion of the people involved, who will be affected by the events in the article and what the effects will be, and so forth. This is a chance for you to get on your soapbox and spout off about something. Have fun with it.

Current Events Rubric

Current Events Rubric	Paper Boy (D)	Writer (C)	Editor (B)	Publisher (A)
Format and Content	Student turned in an article and wrote about it. Or, student turned in a current event complete, but late.	Student turned in an article with the biographical information, a summary, and a reaction.	Student turned in an article and used the complete and proper format to write about the article with a reaction of appropriate length (½ page minimum) and included his or her thoughts on the topic.	Student turned in an article, followed the format, and had a thoughtful response including the student's opinions on the article and the people and events surrounding the story.

Comments: _____

_____

_____

_____

_____

Lesson 2
Newspaper Project

Grade Level: 5–8

Approximate Length of Time: 5–8 hours (classes)

Prerequisite Knowledge:

- The students' work on the current events assignment should prepare them for this project.
- You may want to review the parts of a newspaper, headlines, and the format of newspaper articles.

Rationale: This project allows students to simulate newspaper articles and thereby use the skills stated in the objectives. It allows for student choice and different learning styles.

National Standards Addressed: The content standards covered will depend on the content area for which the assignment is used and the stories the student chooses. The skills addressed are:

- Economics—The student understands the role factors of production play in a society's economy. The student will identify important economic trends and stories.
- Government—The student understands the concept of limited governments, such as constitutional and democratic governments, and unlimited governments, such as totalitarian and nondemocratic governments. The student will identify and report on the status of the government and major news stories dealing with government.
- Social Studies—The student communicates in written, oral, and visual forms. In addition, the student is expected to:
    - use social studies terminology correctly;
    - incorporate main and supporting ideas in verbal and written communication;
    - create written and visual material such as journal entries, reports, graphic organizers, outlines, and bibliographies; and
    - use standard grammar, spelling, sentence structure, and punctuation.

Objectives: Students will be able to:

- work together in small groups to meet deadlines and create a finished project;
- research major news stories, cultural events, recreational events, and businesses from the selected country being studied;
- organize the research into a newspaper format; and
- use a rubric to self-check their assignment.

Materials:

- Internet access
- domestic or foreign language periodicals
- Newspaper Project worksheet (pp. 38–39)
- Newspaper Template (pp. 41–45)
- Newspaper Project Rubric (p. 46)
- glue, scissors, art materials

Procedure:

Opening: This project is great for small groups. It allows students to do research about various countries and produce a creative product for a real-world audience. In this project, students will create a fictional newspaper from a country in the region they are studying. The different jobs in each group require different skills and talents, which readily allow the students to differentiate their learning.

Development of Lesson:

1. Students should be given the Newspaper Project directions, the template, and the rubric. Be sure to go over all the information with the class and answer any questions.
2. Divide the class into groups of 4–6 students. Assign the job responsibilities or have students decide on their duties within their groups.
3. Assign due dates to divide the project into smaller pieces for the students. Examples of due dates include:
   - Three to five sources due by _____.
   - Research completed by _____ .
   - Articles written by _____ .
   - Cartoons and advertisements completed by ___ .
4. Students can glue the articles, ads, and cartoons onto the template provided or use software to create their own newspaper format. If they decide to glue, be sure to run copies for them to make smooth newspapers.

Closure: Have students share their newspapers with other groups.

Assessment: Group newspapers will be assessed, by the teacher, using the Newspaper Project Rubric. Be sure to hand the students a copy of the rubric so that expectations are clear.

Independent Activities/Lesson Extension/Adaptations:

- Have students write letters to the editor of one of the papers created in the class.
- Have students write to a real newspaper editor about a topic of interest found in the paper.
- Visit your local newspaper's offices to learn how a newspaper is developed.

lesson 2
newspaper project

Objective: Your group will produce a newspaper from a nation in the region we are studying. Each person in your group will fulfill at least one of the roles listed below.

Roles:

Editor in chief—This person is in charge of the overall look and layout of the newspaper. This is also the person in charge of setting and enforcing deadlines. The Editor in chief has the ultimate responsibility of making sure the paper gets out on time and has quality information presented in a way that makes people want to read it. It's good to be the king, but there are responsibilities. This role will be filled by _____.

Copy editor—This is the grammar police. This person double-checks the spelling, grammar, and facts of an article. Be sure to have the reporters make the changes. This role will be filled by _____.

Advertising/Sales—This person's job is to determine the size, style, and placement of advertisements. At a real newspaper, they sell the ad space (bigger costs more, color costs more, and placement toward the front page costs more). This is where newspapers make most of their money. The ads should be created by this person and/or other team members. This role will be filled by _____.

Managing Editor: Cartoons—This person decides which cartoons and comics should appear in the paper and where they get placed. In our paper they will also contribute the most artwork and cartoons/comics. This role will be filled by _____.

Printer—This person is in charge of the hardware that prints the paper. After everyone is done with his or her job, the printer will print out a hardcopy of your newspaper. The printer works closely with the Editor in chief to layout the paper and create its look. This role will be filled by _____.

Photographer/Illustrator—This person provides photographs, illustrations, diagrams, and/or charts for the articles. This role will be filled by _____.

Reporter(s)—The reporters write the bulk of the articles. Be sure your newspaper meets the minimum requirements given below. This role will be filled by _____.

Minimum Requirements: Your group's newspaper must have at least these articles. The numbers in parenthesis indicate the minimum number of stories required in each content area. Of course, you may do more if you would like.

1. World news—From your country's perspective. (1)
2. National news—Important events in your country; one about the government and one about the economy. (2)
3. Local news—Important events from the city in which your paper is published. (1)
4. Lifestyle—Entertainment popular in your nation: one about fine arts (orchestra, dance, painting, etc.), and one about popular culture (movies, concerts, TV). (2)
5. Political cartoon(s)—These are editorials in pictures. (1)
6. Advertisements—These should promote and attempt to sell products manufactured in your nation. (2)
7. Sports—Scores and other news about popular sports in the country. (2)
8. Weather map—A national map showing the weather in your nation. Include a key. Also, include the forecast for the next 5 days.
9. Every article, advertisement, and cartoon should include a byline (who wrote or created the piece).
10. Every page should have the date and name of the paper.

Every person in your group should contribute more than one of the above items, as well as perform their job as listed above. Be sure your name appears on everything you contribute.

You may cut and paste onto the templates given on the following pages, or you may use software and print out your newspaper from the computer.

Due dates for the project:

Three to five sources by _____

Articles, advertisements, and cartoons due by_____

Layout completed and agreed upon by_____

Complete newspaper turned in by _____

Name of Newspaper

Date of Issue | Volume #, Issue # | Cost of Newspaper

National News

World News

Lifestyle

Sports

Lead Story HEADLINE . . . HEADLINE . . . HEADLINE . . .

Byline

Lead Story

Lead Story Photo

Cutline . . . Cutline . . . Cutline . . . Cutline . . . Cutline . . .

Photo (for story below)

Cutline . . . Cutline . . . Cutline . . . Cutline . . . Cutline . . .

HEADLINE . . . HEADLINE . . . HEAD-LINE . . . HEADLINE . . .

Byline

Article

(continue story on another page)

HEADLINE . . . HEADLINE . . . HEADLINE . . .

Byline

Article

(continue story on another page, if needed)

Section Title

HEADLINE . . .
HEADLINE . . .
HEADLINE . . .

Byline

Article

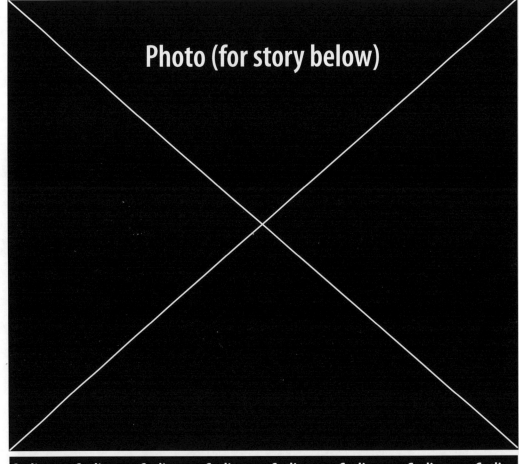

Photo (for story below)

Cutline . . . Cutline . . . Cutline . . . Cutline . . . Cutline . . . Cutline . . . Cutline . . . Cutline . . . Cutline . . . Cutline . . . Cutline . . . Cutline . . . Cutline . . . Cutline . . .

HEADLINE . . . HEADLINE . . . HEADLINE . . . HEAD-LINE . . . HEADLINE . . . HEADLINE . . . HEADLINE . .

Byline

Article

Weather Page Title

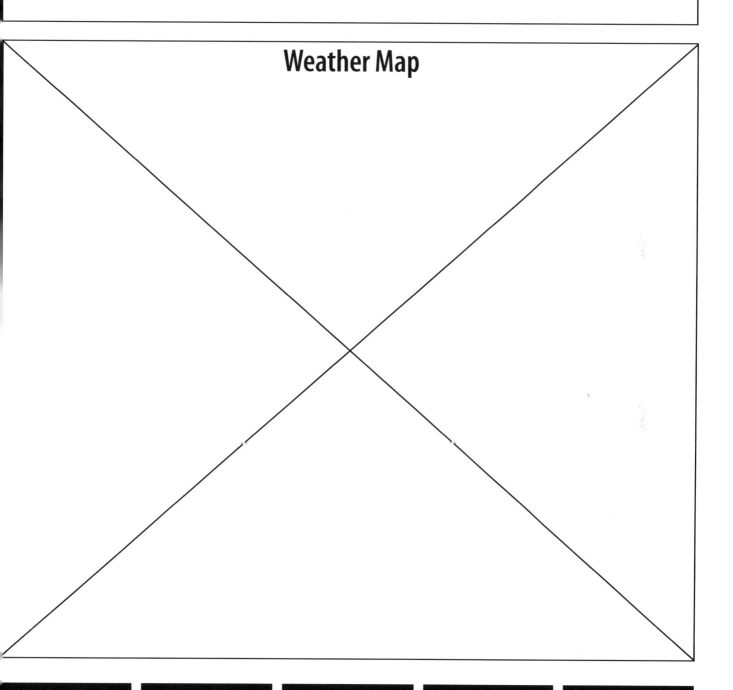

Weather Map

Five Day Forecast	Five Day Forecast	Five Day Forecast	Five Day Forecast	Five Day Forecast

Section Title

HEADLINE . . . HEADLINE

Byline

Article

HEADLINE . . . HEADLINE . . . HEADLINE .
HEADLINE . . . HEADLINE . . . HEADLINE .

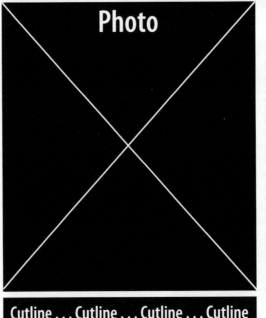

Photo

Byline

Article

Cutline . . . Cutline . . . Cutline . . . Cutline
. . . Cutline . . . Cutline . . . Cutline

HEADLINE . . . HEADLINE
HEADLINE . . . HEADLINE

Byline

Article

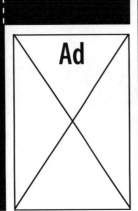

Ad

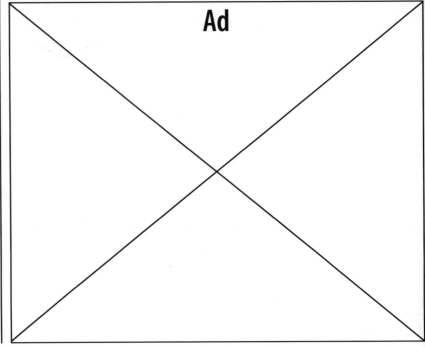

Ad

Section Title

HEADLINE . . . HEADLINE . . . HEADLINE . . . HEADLINE . . . HEADLINE . .

Byline

Article

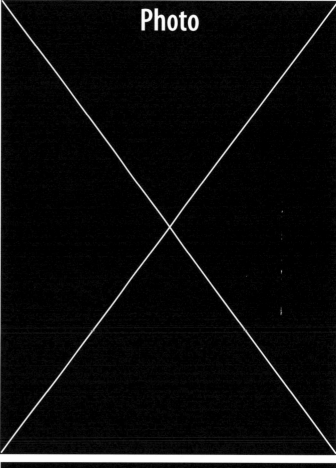
Photo

Cutline . . . Cutline . . . Cutline . . . Cutline . . . Cutline

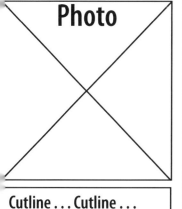
Photo

Cutline . . . Cutline . . .

HEADLINE . . . HEADLINE . . . HEADLINE . . .

Byline

Article

Newspaper Project Rubric

Newspaper Project Rubric	*National Inquirer* (D)	Local Paper (C)	*USA Today* (B)	*New York Times* (A)
Content	The group turned in a project	The group turned in a project that meets the minimum requirements with articles from a country in the region studied.	The group turned in a project that exceeds the minimum requirements in quality, with well-written articles. The majority of the articles are realistic and current.	The group accomplished all the standards for *USA Today* and a reader will learn useful and pertinent information about the subject nation.
Format	The layout is confusing to the reader and the articles and ads are difficult to read.	The layout is confusing to the reader.	The layout is organized and easy to decipher.	The newspaper is creatively designed and well put together.
Group Work	The group did not complete the project on time.	Less than half of the members of the group did much more than half of the work.	The group worked well together with a fair division of labor.	The group worked well together with all members contributing equally.

Comments: _____

_____

_____

_____

_____

Lesson 3
Radio News

Grade Level: 5–8

Approximate Length of Time: 10 hours

Prerequisite Knowledge:

- Mass media experience from previous projects.

Rationale: This project allows students to simulate a radio news show and thereby use the skills stated in the objectives. It allows for student choice and different learning styles. This project takes the skills from the previous projects and brings them into a new medium. New technology is required to fulfill the requirements.

National Standards Addressed:

- Economics—The student understands the role factors of production play in a society's economy. The student will identify important economic trends and stories.
- Government—The student understands the concept of limited governments, such as constitutional and democratic governments, and unlimited governments, such as totalitarian and nondemocratic governments. The student will identify and report on the status of the government and major news stories dealing with government.
- Social Studies—The student communicates in written, oral, and visual forms. In addition, the student is expected to:
  - use social studies terminology correctly,
  - incorporate main and supporting ideas in verbal and written communication, and
  - express ideas orally based on research and experiences.

Objectives: Students will be able to:

- produce their own radio show from the point of view of the nation they are studying;
- fulfill group roles and meet deadlines;
- research major news stories, cultural events, recreational events, and businesses from the country selected; and
- use a rubric to self-check their assignment.

Materials:

- radio
- tape recorder
- Internet access
- domestic and international periodicals

Procedure:

Opening: This lesson takes the skills and knowledge gained from the Newspaper Project and transfers it to a new medium: radio. This time students will record a radio news show based in the region they are studying. This project is for small groups. Like the Newspaper Project, it requires real research and has real-world application and connections. If students chose their roles for the last project, the teacher should assign roles for this one, and vice versa.

Development of Lesson:

1. Students should be asked to listen to a radio news show. Local morning drive time shows on talk radio or your local NPR affiliate will be the most helpful. Let the students hear some of the show uninterrupted. It is a good idea to assign this as homework.

   Now ask the students to pay closer attention to some of the details in the formatting of the show. The teacher should lead a discussion of how a radio news show is done. Use the Newspaper Project as a reference. The discussion should include questions such as: What is a teaser? Do the stories have headlines? What is the purpose of the headline/title of a piece? Are the stories presented in a particular order (national, international, local, weather, sports, culture)? Why are they ordered that way? How is the format like a newspaper? How is it different?

2. Now have the students listen to the radio news show again.

3. Hand students the Radio Show Project directions and the rubric. Go over the information with the class and answer any questions.

4. Divide the students into groups of 4–6 students. Assign the roles or have students decide on roles.

5. Assign due dates. Some examples of due dates include:
   - Three to five sources by _____
   - Three to five sound effects, dialogue, or bits of music by _____
   - Script for stories by _____
   - Script for host/anchor by _____
   - Completed tape turned in by _____

6. There are a number of ways students can create the tapes. They can get together and read the scripts while recording and have the engineer play the sound bites in real time; they can all record their parts and the engineer can put them all together on one tape; or there is some great sound editing software available.

Closure: Tapes should be played for the class and wrap-up worksheets should be completed.

Assessment: This project will be graded by the teacher, according to the Radio Show Rubric. Be sure to give students a copy so that expectations are clear.

Independent Activities/Lesson Extension/Adaptations:

- Visit a local radio station.
- Listen to radio shows (news, comedy, serials) from the early to mid-1900s.
- Discuss the impact of early radio on society and popular culture.

lesson 3
radio show program

Directions: You are going to produce a radio news program. You will make an audio recording of your show (tape or disk) to be heard by the class. Your show will be based in a country we have been studying.

Our country is _____

There are different roles for the people in your group to fill. Everyone should help complete all the tasks.

Roles:

Producer—The producer is in charge of the content and getting a quality show on the air on time. This role will be filled by

_____.

Anchor(s)—The anchor is the person who ties all the pieces together. They introduce each story and give quick headlines for the day (which may or may not be the subject of stories covered more in-depth by reporters). This role will be filled by

_____.

Reporters—These are the people "in the field." They write their stories and deliver them on air. These roles will be filled by

_____.

Engineer(s)—This is the person in charge of the technical side. They find the sound effects and/or bits of speeches or dialogue and insert them into the stories. They then dub the final show together. This role will be filled by _____.

Stories:
You show must contain stories from the following content areas, and remember, your show is from the country assigned. The numbers in parenthesis are the minimum number of stories required in each content area. Of course, you may do more if you prefer.

1. National news—The big stories from your country. (2)
2. International news—The headlines from around the world. (2)
3. Local—News affecting the city in which your show is located. (1)
4. Culture—The fine arts events taking place in your city. (1)
5. Sports—Scores and highlights from your area. (1)
6. Weather—The forecast for the day of your show and the week ahead.

Format:

There are many different ways to deliver the news on the radio. Your group needs to decide which type you are going to use.

There are serious news shows that truly seek to do in-depth reporting along with entertaining pieces. NPR (National Public Radio) or PRI (Public Radio International) are good examples.

There are drive time shows that have two subgroups: talk radio and music radio. Talk radio tends to be more like the serious shows, but may be slanted toward one political view. The other type is what you hear on a regular FM station in the morning and during the evening rush-hour. They are lighter and funnier with more serious stories handled by a newsperson rather than the anchors who are more concerned with entertainment.

Listen to all these types and decide which best fits your group. Remember, your show has to be informative, and must contain the minimum number of required stories as listed above.

Due Dates:

Three to five sources by _____

Three to five sound effects, dialogue, or bits of music by

_____

Script for stories by _____

Script for host/anchor by _____

Completed tape turned in by _____

Radio Show Rubric

Radio Show Rubric	Intern (D)	Field Reporter (C)	Weekend Anchor (B)	Drive-time Anchor (A)
Content	The show included facts from the country studied.	The show included many accurate facts about the country studied.	Every piece in the show included accurate and interesting facts from the country.	Every piece included accurate and interesting facts and the show felt like it came from the country, rather than being about the country.
Presentation	A completed tape was turned in.	All the due dates were met and the project met the minimum requirements.	All the due dates were met and the group had good ideas and a well put-together show.	All the due dates were met, all instructions were followed, and a creative show was produced with very few mistakes or problems.
Group Work	The group did not complete the assignment on time.	Less than half of the members of the group did more than half of the work.	The group worked well together with a fair division of labor.	The group worked very well together with all members contributing equally.

Comments: _____

_____

_____

_____

Lesson 4
TV News Show

Grade Level: 5–8

Approximate Length of Time: 10 hours

Prerequisite Knowledge:

- Impact of TV on American culture.
- Knowledge and skills gained from previous projects.

Rationale: This project allows students to simulate a TV news show and thereby use the skills stated in the objectives. It allows for student choice and different learning styles. New technology is needed to fulfill the requirements.

National Standards Addressed:

- Economics—The student understands the role factors of production play in a society's economy. The student will identify important economic trends and stories.
- Government—The student understands the concept of limited governments, such as constitutional and democratic governments, and unlimited governments, such as totalitarian and nondemocratic governments. The student will identify and report on the status of the government and major news stories dealing with government.
- Social Studies—In addition, the student communicates in written, oral, and visual forms. The student is expected to:
  - use social studies terminology correctly,
  - incorporate main and supporting ideas in verbal and written communication, and
  - express ideas orally based on research and experiences.

Objectives: Students will be able to:

- produce their TV news show from the point of view of the nation they are studying;
- fulfill group roles and meet deadlines;
- research major news stories, cultural events, recreational events, and businesses from the country selected; and
- use a rubric to self-check their assignment.

Materials:

- TV, VCR and /or DVD player
- camcorder
- recorded TV news shows
- video editing software and computer (optional)

Procedure:

Opening: This lesson builds on what the students learned in the other lessons and the skills they have practiced. Now, they put those ideas to work in the medium they know best, television. The students will produce a TV news show. The traditional local news show format works best, using one or two anchors who introduce stories and give quick summaries and then send the viewer out to other reporters who cover more in-depth and/or specialized stories.

Development of Lesson:

1. Students should be asked to watch a local TV news show. This may be assigned as homework.

2. After the students have watched the local news show, tell them you want them to pay closer attention to some of the details in the formatting of the show. The teacher should lead a discussion of how a TV news show is organized. Use the Newspaper Project and Radio Project as references. The discussion should include questions such as: What is a teaser? Do the stories have headlines? What is the purpose of the headline/title of a piece? Are the stories presented in a particular order (national, international, local, weather, sports, culture)? Why are they ordered that way? How is the format like a newspaper? How is it different? How is it similar and different from a radio show?

3. Have the students watch the show again, keeping in mind the discussion they had in class.

4. Hand students the TV News Show Project directions and the rubric. Go over the information with the class and answer any questions.

5. Divide the students into groups of 4–6 students. Assign the roles or have students decide on roles.

6. Assign due dates. Some examples of due dates include:
   - Three to five sources by _____
   - Set decorations, props, and graphics by _____
   - Script for stories by _____
   - Script for host/anchor by _____
   - Completed tape turned in by _____

7. The shows should be taped during one or two class periods. Set up an anchor desk and some other news desks around the room. The groups can set up their props and set decorations and then record their show. It usually works best if the teacher works the camera. If your school has a multimedia lab, the teacher or the students can edit the pieces to make them look more professional (e.g., graphics, fade-ins, etc.)

Closure: Shows should be aired for the class and wrap-up worksheets should be completed.

Assessment: This project will be graded using the wrap-up worksheets, and by the teacher, using the TV News Show Rubric. Be sure to hand students the rubric so that expectations are clear.

Independent Activities/Lesson Extension/Adaptations:

- Visit a local television station to see a news broadcast or to talk with the anchors.
- Discuss the role of TV news in our society.
- Discuss bias in the media.

lesson 4
wrap-up worksheet

This worksheet is to be completed after you have experienced a group's Radio Show and TV News Show. Review the directions for this project and the rubric.

Score the group in the following categories using a four-point scale.
1 = poor (They did not do what was expected; they have a lot of work to do.)
2 = needs improvement (They need to put more effort into this area.)
3 = satisfactory (They did a good job.)
4 = excellent (They did something special that surprised you with how good it was.)

Entertainment—Did you enjoy their show?

1   2   3   4

Organization—Did the show appear to be well planned out and rehearsed?

1   2   3   4

Content—Did you learn a lot about the country the show was set in?

1   2   3   4

What was the best part of the show?

What needed the most improvement?

What are three things you learned about the country in which the show was set?

1.

2.

3.

TV News Show Rubric

TV News Show Rubric	Local Evening News (D)	Nightline (C)	CNN (B)	60 Minutes (A)
Content	The show included facts from the country studied.	The show included many accurate facts about the country studied.	Every piece in the show included accurate and interesting facts from the country.	Every piece included accurate and interesting facts and the show felt like it came from the country, rather than being about the country.
Presentation	The group made a TV news show.	All the due dates were met and the project met the minimum requirements.	All the due dates were met and the group had good ideas and a well put-together show.	All the due dates were met, all instructions were followed, and a creative show was produced with very few mistakes or problems.
Group Work	The group did not complete the assignment on time.	Less than half the members of the group did more than half of the work.	The group worked well together with a fair division of labor.	The group worked very well together with all members contributing equally.

Comments: _____

_____

_____

_____

_____

Magnificent Mascots!
–Developed by Jessica Fell

Unit Overview: The unit examines adaptation through individual survival characteristics within a species, adaptive characteristics of different species, and the comparison of existing and past species. The unit will use Problem-Based Learning (PBL) as a basis for enrichment of the existing curriculum. Students will develop knowledge and skills centered around adaptation through the introductory lessons. Students will be presented with a Unit Problem (selecting a class mascot), and students will work in groups to solve the problem.

Resources Needed: (These resources are recommended, not mandatory.)

- *Ice Age Cave Bear: The Giant Beast That Terrified Ancient Humans* by Barbara Hehner, illustrated by Mark Hallett, 2002, ISBN# 0-37582-194-5
- *Ice Age Sabertooth: The Most Ferocious Cat That Ever Lived* by Barbara Hehner, illustrated by Mark Hallett, 2002, ISBN# 0-37582-193-7
- *What Do You Do When Something Wants To Eat You?* by Steve Jenkins, 1997, ISBN# 0-61815-243-1
- *Animal Defenses: How Animals Protect Themselves* by Etta Kaner, illustrated by Pat Stephens, 1999, ISBN# 1-55074-419-4

Helpful Resources:

- Scholastic (Animal Adaptation)—http://teacher.scholastic.com/dirtrep/animal
- Family Education Network (Animal Adaptation)—http://www.teachervision.fen.com/tv/curriculum/weeklywebadventures/animal_adapt/t_home.html
- Utah Education Network (Animal Adaptation)—http://www.uen.org/utahlink/activities/view_activity.cgi?activity_id=4750
- *When Mammoths Walked the Earth* by Caroline Arnold, illustrated by Laurie Caple, 2002, ISBN# 0-61809-633-7
- *Poisoners and Pretenders* by Michael Chinery, 2000, ISBN# 0-61328-024-5
- *Prehistoric Animals* by Daniel Cohen, illustrated by Pamela Ford Johnson, 1988, ISBN# 038523-417-1
- *What are Camouflage and Mimicry?* by Bobby Kalman, and John Crossingham, 2001, ISBN# 0-86505-962-4

- *Fur, Feathers, and Flippers: How Animals Live Where They Do* by Patricia Lauber, 1994, ISBN# 0-59045-071-9
- *Prehistoric Mammals* by Anne McCord, illustrated by Bob Hersey, 1977, ISBN# 0-88110-120-6
- *Animal Magicians: Mystery and Magic of the Animal World* by David Taylor, 1989, ISBN# 0-82252-175-X
- *Animal Olympians: Sporting Champions of the Animal World* by David Taylor, 1989, ISBN# 0-82252-177-6
- *How Animals Live: The Amazing World of Animals in the Wild* by Bernard Stonehouse, and Esther Bertram, and illustrated by John Francis, 2004, ISBN# 0-43954-834-9

Lesson 1
Introducing: Adaptation!

Grade Level: 4

Approximate Length of Time: 2 classes (45–60 minutes each)

Rationale: This lesson will allow students to create their own definition of the term *adaptation*. It also introduces the adaptive characteristics of animals. Students will use this background information throughout the unit to study adaptation.

National Standard Addressed: The students will compare adaptive characteristics of various species.

Objectives: Students will be able to:

- define adaptation, and
- list eight animals and each of the animal's adaptive characteristics.

Materials:

- *What Do You Do When Something Wants to Eat You?* by Steve Jenkins
- *Animal Defenses: How Animals Protect Themselves* by Etta Kaner
- a variety of books and resources for research
- What Makes Me Special worksheet (p. 64).

Procedure:

Opening: Read *What Do You Do When Something Wants to Eat You?* to the class. Or, read *Animal Defenses: How Animals Protect Themselves* to the class. Lead a question and answer period and class discussion on the book's content. Introduce the term *adaptation* and have the class brainstorm definitions of adaptation.

Development of Lesson:

1. At this point, the students should be divided into groups of 3–5 students for research. The groups can be teacher selected or selected through topic interests (introduce the topic as animal research and let students group together in animal groups or groups of interest— e.g., mammals and amphibians). Instruct students that they will be researching animals and they should bring in any resources they would like to share for the next class.

2. Second class period: Review the definition of adaptation (write the students' definition on the board or on a poster in the room).

3. Instruct the students that they will be researching the adaptive characteristics of eight different animals.

4. Model an animal and the animal's adaptive characteristics with the class on the board.

5. Provide as many resources as possible so that students have a variety of animals to choose from and many sources to find information.

6. Observe as groups research and complete the What Makes Me Special worksheet.

Closure: When the groups have researched eight different animals, have each student share a new fact with the class. They could each have a sticky note and write the animal and the animal's adaptive characteristic on the note. Each student could read their note as they stick it to the wall or on the board. Encourage students to share information that may be new to the rest of the class.

Assessment: Record participation in groups on a checklist or annotated notes. Evaluate the presentation of the new animal fact. Evaluate the What Makes Me Special worksheet for completion (eight animals) and content (adaptive characteristics are accurate).

Independent Activities/Lesson Extension/Adaptations:

- Students may fill out chart paper after or instead of the worksheet and present to the class.
- Students may bring worksheets home to further investigate the topic. They may also choose to do more than eight animals.
- One person can record information while the group researches and dictates.

lesson 1
what makes me special?

Animal	Adaptive Characteristics
1.	
2.	
3.	
4.	
5.	
6.	
7.	
8.	

Lesson 2
Prehistoric Connections

Grade Level: 4

Approximate Length of Time: 1–2 lessons (45–60 minutes each)

Rationale: This lesson will introduce prehistoric animals to students, and students will compare prehistoric species to species that exist today. Students will utilize compare and contrast skills to learn about adaptation and prehistoric animals.

National Standard Addressed: The students will identify the kinds of species that lived in the past and compare them to existing species.

Objectives: Students will be able to:

- discuss prehistoric animals and extinction, and
- compare prehistoric and living species.

Materials:

- *Ice Age Cave Bear: The Giant Bear That Terrified Ancient Humans* by Barbara Hehner
- *Ice Age Sabertooth: The Most Ferocious Cat That Ever Lived* by Barbara Hehner
- a variety of books and resources for research
- Prehistoric Connections worksheet (p. 68)
- poster or picture of a prehistoric animal

Procedure:

Opening: Introduce topic by displaying a poster or picture of a prehistoric animal (if necessary, show the cover of a book). Ask students if they can name the animal, and if they know anything about the animal.

Discuss the features of the animal and ask students if they know when it lived and if it is still alive. Explain that the animal is extinct and ask students to think of reasons why the animal is extinct. Brainstorm with students on the board.

Development of Lesson:

1. Ask students if they think the animal they have just seen resembles a modern day animal. If so, which animal does it resemble, and why are they the same and why are they different? Introduce resources with prehistoric animals and hand out worksheet.
2. Divide students into groups to research prehistoric animals (the teacher can select the groups or students can select their groups based on the animal they want to research).
3. Instruct students that they will choose a prehistoric animal and compare it to a modern animal that they think it resembles. They will

then fill out the Prehistoric Connections worksheet comparing the two animals.

Closure: Groups will present the comparison charts they completed (for this exercise the group can transfer information onto chart paper if they like). Discuss other examples of modern animals that resemble prehistoric animals that they came across in their research.

Assessment: Record participation in class and small groups on a checklist or annotated notes. Evaluate the Prehistoric Connections worksheet for content. Evaluate group presentations using the Group Presentation Rubric.

Independent Activities/Lesson Extension/Adaptations:

- If possible, it would be beneficial to work with other classrooms and have some classrooms select prehistoric animals as their mascots. This would help create the Unit Problem and create additional resources for students.
- Students may want to extend the lesson to further research the prehistoric animals and the concept of extinction.
- Instead of completing the worksheet, one student can record information onto chart paper, and the whole group can research and present their information together.

lesson 2
prehistoric connections

	Prehistoric Animal	Modern Animal
What is my name?		
What is the same?		
What is different?		
Interesting facts . . .		

lesson 2
group presentation rubric

Group Participants _____

Content

3   The content was informative, well-researched, and relevant.

2   The content was informative

1   The content was interesting but not well-researched.

0   The content was not interesting or well-researched.

Organization

3   The presentation and materials were well organized.

2   The presentation was organized.

1   The presentation was organized but the materials were not.

0   The presentation and materials were not organized.

Verbal Skills

3   The students spoke clearly and presented with exemplary verbal skills.

2   The students spoke clearly.

1   The students presented but did not demonstrate strong verbal skills.

0   The students did not present.

Nonverbal Skills

3   The students demonstrated exemplary nonverbal skills both as presenters and as audience members.

2   The students demonstrated exemplary nonverbal skills as presenters or as audience members.

1   The students demonstrated satisfactory nonverbal skills as presenters or as audience members.

0   The students demonstrated unsatisfactory nonverbal skills as presenters and as audience members.

Total   /12

Lesson 3
My Mascot

Grade Level: 4

Approximate Length of Time: 1 2 classes (45 60 minutes each)

Rationale: This lesson allows students to utilize the information, knowledge, resources, and skills obtained from the previous lessons in this unit to select an animal to represent them as their mascot.

National Standards Addressed: The students will identify the kinds of species that lived in the past and compare them to existing species. The students will compare adaptive characteristics of various species.

Objectives: Students will be able to:

- select a mascot based on criteria from the Unit Problem, and
- outline the adaptive characteristics of the selected animal.

Materials:

- a variety of books and resources for research
- Unit Problem handout (p. 72)
- My Mascot worksheet (p. 73)
- What Makes Me Special worksheet for reference

Procedure:

Opening: Review previous lessons with a class discussion. Highlight the student definition of adaptation and the comparisons of prehistoric and existing species. Ask students why they think animals changed or adapted. Introduce and hand out the Unit Problem to students.

Development of Lesson:

1. Instruct students to use the What Makes Me Special worksheet to select one animal that they think has the best survival skills to be their mascot.

2. The students should further research the selected animal and complete the My Mascot handout. Emphasize that the students will need information about their animal and its adaptive characteristics in order to defend their selection.

Closure: Each group announces what animal they believe will make the best class mascot. Their animal is now the name of their group. Students should be encouraged to bring in any materials or resources related to these animals.

Assessment: Record research participation in groups on a checklist or annotated notes. Evaluate the My Mascot worksheet for completion and content (adaptive characteristics are accurate).

Independent Activities/Lesson Extension/Adaptations:

- This is a great opportunity to bring in a classroom theme. If students are divided into tables or groups already, shift them so that they sit with their research groups. When students name their mascot this can become their group name. These groups/names can be used for group points (classroom management) and group teams for PE.
- Although the focus of this unit is adaptation, encourage students to become experts on their animals and learn about reproduction, habitat, and related topics.
- If possible, any field trips related to animals and adaptation would be beneficial. Aquariums and zoos are excellent resources, especially if you inform them of your class topic.

activity 3
unit problem
Our class needs a mascot!

All the other classes in the school have chosen prehistoric animals to represent them. We want a mascot that will adapt, survive, and reproduce successfully, unlike the extinct animals chosen by other classes.

Our mascot must demonstrate extreme survival skills to represent the competitive nature of our classroom spirit.

You must select and design a mascot that demonstrates characteristics that will help it survive above all other animals.

What animal should represent our class and what should it look like?

lesson 3
my mascot

Animal

_____

Adaptive Characteristics

_____

_____

_____

_____

_____

_____

_____

_____

_____

_____

_____

_____

_____

Lesson 4
The Great Debate

Grade Level: 4

Approximate Length of Time: 1 class (45–60 minutes)

Rationale: This lesson allows students to utilize the information, knowledge, resources, and skills obtained from the previous lessons in this unit to select an animal that they want to represent them as class mascot. The lesson will allow students to learn and practice debate skills in order to defend their selection process.

National Standard Addressed: The students will compare adaptive characteristics of various species.

Objectives: Students will be able to:

- use information gathered in previous lessons to debate the adaptive characteristics their animal and whether or not it should be the class mascot.

Materials:

- previous worksheets for reference: What Makes Me Special and My Mascot
- a stopwatch or egg timer
- Debate Scorecard worksheet (p. 76)

Procedure:

Opening: Review the animals that each group selected to be the class mascot. Outline or review the rules of a debate using the Debate Scorecard worksheet. (Each group has 1 minute to make a statement and the other group has 2 minutes to respond. One person speaks at a time. Points are awarded for the most convincing group at the end of a response. The debate is over after a set time limit. No negative or disrespectful comments).
Development of Lesson:
1. Randomly pick groups to debate each other.
2. Instruct the students that they are to debate the "survival skills" of their animal compared to the other group's animal. Each group member must participate in the debate.

Closure: Once each group has had the opportunity to debate their animal, tally up the points from the debates. Announce the animal that "won" the debate and thus far demonstrates extreme survival skills. At this point congratulate students on the appropriateness of their behavior during the debates or comment on the success of the class debates.

Assessment: Record participation in debate on a checklist or annotated notes (each student needs to contribute/participate). Evaluate students based on participation, debate behavior (audience skills), and debate content.

Independent Activities/Lesson Extension/Adaptations:

- Inviting other classes, teachers, or audience members might be exciting for the debaters. It is crucial that audience members are respectful participants and follow the rules of the debate.
- Those students who are afraid to participate during the debate can arrange a speaker on their behalf, but they must present the content to you before the debate.
- Debate points can be added to group points if this is a classroom management technique in the classroom.
- Allow students to present video clips or resources with their animals before the debate.

activity 4
debate scorecard

Award one point per round.

Each round has one statement (1 minute) and one response (2 minutes).

Each group starts with 5 points that can be deducted due to poor debate behavior or poor audience behavior.

Groups with the most points at the end of the debates win.

Animal   Animal

_____   VS   _____

Points: Points:

_____   _____

Animal   Animal

_____   VS   _____

Points: Points:

_____   _____

Animal   Animal

_____   VS   _____

Points: Points:

_____   _____

Animal   Animal

_____   VS   _____

Points: Points:

_____   _____

Lesson 5
Making Mascots

Grade Level: 4

Approximate Length of Time: 2 classes (45–60 minutes each)

Rationale: This lesson will allow students to create a class mascot based on their previous knowledge of adaptation and adaptive characteristics. The lesson encourages students to analyze the Unit Problem as a group and create a viable solution without outside influence. The lesson also encourages the use of multiple or innovative mediums that encourage independent thought and creative solutions.

National Standard Addressed: The students will identify characteristics that allow members within a species to survive and reproduce.

Objectives: Students will be able to:

- create mascots based on the criteria from the Unit Problem, and
- select a medium to create their mascot.

Materials:

- a variety of books and resources for research
- previous worksheets for reference: What Makes Me Special, Unit Problem, and My Mascot
- examples of animal mascots (posters, jerseys, merchandise, etc.)
- variety of materials for the creation of a mascot (writing utensils, paper, clay, paints, fabric, and computers with graphic design programs).

Procedure:

Opening: Introduce lesson by displaying different examples of mascots to the class. If possible use some examples of prehistoric animals.

Development of Lesson:

1. Ask students to define the word *mascot* and write down the student definition on the board or on poster paper. Ask students if they can list examples of animal mascots.

2. Brainstorm on the board. What would help their mascots survive better than other animals in the same species? Ask students why the mascot they create should be the best (or have the most adaptive characteristics) of the species.

3. Read the Unit Problem to the students again and ask them if they have any questions about the problem.

4. Instruct students that as a group they are to create an animal mascot using their choice of medium. They must follow the instructions and criteria from the Unit Problem sheet.

5.   Give students ample time, materials, and mediums to create their mascot.

Closure: At the conclusion of the work periods, ask students to share with the class the medium that they have chosen to create the mascot and how the project is progressing. Explain that the mascots are not to be displayed yet, but unveiled to voters later.

Assessment:
Record participation in groups on a checklist or annotated notes. Evaluate the mascots based on creativity, use of their selected medium, accuracy (are the features of the animal correct?), and animal characteristics (does the animal demonstrate characteristics that would allow it to survive and reproduce?).

Independent Activities/Lesson Extension/Adaptations:

- Students may choose to create the mascot from materials that are unavailable at school. Allow class time to plan the mascot and allow students to take their work home.
- Leave the project open and instead of having students explain their medium and progress, ask them to highlight characteristics of their mascot.
- Invite a local mascot to introduce the lesson. Look into inviting mascots from local universities, recreation centers, or businesses.
- Each student could create their own mascot.

activity 5
mascot evaluation

Name_____   Date_____

	Beginning 1	Developing 2	Accomplished 3	Exemplary 4	Score
Creativity	There are no original representations of other examples	Attempt to use original ideas	Original ideas are displayed	Inventive and original ideas are displayed	
Use of Medium	Medium selection based on availability or ease	Medium selection based on availability or ease but utilized effectively	Purposeful selection or utilization of medium	Purposeful selection and utilization of medium	
Accuracy	The animal's features are not accurate	Some of the animal's features are accurate	Mascot demonstrates knowledge of the animal's characteristics	Mascot demonstrates knowledge of the animal and the animal's features are accurate	
Animal Characteristics	The mascot may or may not display an adaptive characteristic	The mascot displays at least one adaptive characteristic	The mascot displays some adaptive characteristics	The mascot displays multiple, highlighted adaptive characteristics	

Total   /16

Lesson 6
And the Winner Is . . .

Grade Level: 4

Approximate Length of Time: 1 class (45 60 minutes)

Rationale: This lesson allows students to present the knowledge and skills that they have developed throughout the unit as a political platform. The presentation of the mascot represents the culmination of the unit on adaptation, as well as the student's solution to the Unit Problem. The lesson also introduces democracy and the voting process through practical application.

National Standards Addressed: The students will identify the kinds of species that lived in the past and compare them to existing species. The students will compare adaptive characteristics of various species. The students will identify characteristics that allow members within a species to survive and reproduce.

Objectives: Students will be able to:

- present their completed mascots as candidates for the class mascot, and
- vote for and decide on the mascot that best represents them as a class.

Materials:

- previous worksheets: Unit Problem and My Mascot
- student created mascots
- ballots

Procedure:

Opening: Tell the class that today they are going to present their mascot creations and choose which mascot they feel best represents their class.

Development of Lesson:

1. Explain the procedure for voting to students. If possible, it's best to invite other classes or teachers to participate in the voting process to ensure an unbiased vote.
2. Have each group present their candidate for class mascot. Each group should explain at this time why their mascot is superior to all others. Students can use the My Mascot worksheet in outlining the mascot's adaptive characteristics.
3. Allow voters to view all mascots.
4. Have all participants vote using ballots (simple checklists with the mascot animals listed).
5. Have groups display their mascots and answer voters' questions while the votes are being tabulated.
6. Share the results of the vote with the class.

Closure: Present the winning mascot that received the most votes. Review the adaptive characteristics of the animal that demonstrate survival skills. Emphasize the characteristics of the mascot that would help it survive above all others in the same species. Inform the students that this is now the new class mascot.

Assessment: Record participation in the mascot presentation on a checklist or annotated notes. Evaluate based on accuracy of information and criteria from Unit Problem handout. Evaluate on presentation skills using the Group Presentation Rubric. Groups should all complete self-evaluation and peer-evaluations.

Independent Activities/Lesson Extension/Adaptations:

- It is important to adopt the class mascot that the students vote for. Including the mascot in a variety of activities will validate the students' work. If possible, continue to use the animal groups for the students and display all the mascots.
- Have students dress like their animals for the presentation and vote.
- Students can create an informational poster (like a political platform) for their mascots.
- Present the winner of the vote or the new class mascot at a school assembly.
- If other classes cannot vote on the mascots, present them all in an art gallery format for viewing (this is especially exciting for primary classes).
- Those students who are afraid to present can arrange a speaker on their behalf, but they must present the content to you before the presentation.

lesson 6
group representation rubric

Group Participants _____

Content

3   The content was informative, well-researched, and relevant.

2   The content was informative

1   The content was interesting but not well-researched.

0   The content was not interesting or well-researched.

Organization

3   The presentation and materials were well organized.

2   The presentation was organized.

1   The presentation was organized but the materials were not.

0   The presentation and materials were not organized.

Verbal Skills

3   The students spoke clearly and presented with exemplary verbal skills.

2   The students spoke clearly.

1   The students presented but did not demonstrate strong verbal skills.

0   The students did not present.

Nonverbal Skills

3   The students demonstrated exemplary nonverbal skills both as presenters and as audience members.

2   The students demonstrated exemplary nonverbal skills as presenters or as audience members.

1   The students demonstrated satisfactory nonverbal skills as presenters or as audience members.

0   The students demonstrated unsatisfactory nonverbal skills as presenters and as audience members.

Total   /12

lesson 6
peer and self-evaluation

Directions: Put a check mark in the column that best describes your participation in your group.

	Yes	Sometimes	No
I asked questions when there was something I didn't understand.			
I helped the people in my group.			
I did my best work.			
I worked quietly and stayed on task.			
My part of the presentation was complete.			

Sir Face: A Look at the Surface of Shapes

–Developed by Diana Brigham

Unit Overview: This is an interdisciplinary unit combining math, language arts, and history activities. Students work with two-dimensional shapes to create a castle, and then use their imagination and creativity to create three-dimensional objects in and around the castle. Extensions in math, reading, writing, and language arts are provided. Open-ended activities include story problems, activity tasks, and writing or higher level activities. Each activity builds upon itself as the castle is built and decorated. The final product is a medieval castle covered with geometric shapes.

Resources Needed:

- Computer/Internet Resources
- Terms for Review handout (see p. 131)
- Examples of two- and three-dimensional objects
- Visuals and knowledge of angles, perimeter, and area
- Copies of unit worksheets
- Paper, pencils, art supplies

Helpful Resources:

- http://games.yahoo.com/games/rules/dominoes/gameplay.html
- http://www.aaamath.com/B/g318_px1.htm
- http://www.castles-of-britain.com
- http://www.medieval-castles.net
- http://www.yourchildlearns.com/castle_history.htm
- http://www.newyorkcarver.com/castles.htm
- http://www.infoplease.com
- http://www.disney.com
- http://math.rice.edu/~lanius/Lessons
- http://www.funbrain.com

Lesson 1
Making the Castle Box!

Grade Level: 2–4

Approximate Length of Time: 2–3 hours

Prerequisite Knowledge:

- Terms for review: two dimensions, three dimensions, right angle, perpendicular lines, perimeter, area, line segment, face, side, rectangular prism, pyramid
- Knowledge of how to measure the perimeter and area of objects.
- Students should practice folding paper into a crisp, straight fold on hard-to-fold paper or cardstock using a ruler.

Rationale: Students will utilize measurement and their knowledge of two- and three-dimensional figures to draw line segments. Students will cut and/or fold those lines to create their castle box.

National Standards Addressed:

- The student selects and uses appropriate units and procedures to measure length and area.
- The student identifies and describes lines, shapes, and solids.
- The student applies measurement concepts to solve problems connected to everyday experiences.
- The student selects and uses writing processes in various forms.
- The student selects and uses writing processes for self-initiated and assigned writing

Objectives: Students will be able to:

- use a ruler to create straight lines on a piece of 12" x 18" tag or poster board in the form of a rectangle (demonstrating use of right angles);
- analyze geometric characteristics;
- construct a rectangular-shaped box; and
- write a set of directions for building a pyramid.

Materials:

- worksheets for Lesson #1
- precut 12" x 18" piece of tag board or poster board
- glue, tape, paper clips
- 15-inch rulers
- pencils and art supplies

Procedure:

Opening: In a class discussion, discuss geometric terms from the Terms for Review handout. Students should have a good understanding of these terms prior to proceeding with the unit. Using a ruler, students should practice drawing straight lines and folding paper. Students should draw two line segments on paper to form a 90 degree angle and practice folding the lines to create a corner. Repeat this activity with heavier paper.

Motivational or Introductory Approach: "Today, we are going to use perimeter, right angles, and geometry to build a castle." Complete the story problems on the Lesson 1 worksheet as a class or individually.

Development of Lesson:

1. The teacher will pass out tag board or poster board, precut to 12" x 18". Each student should use this as his or her beginning standard dimensions.

2. Brainstorm information about rectangular prisms, where they are found, and how they are used in real life. Make a list as a class or have students work independently. Read the list aloud and ask for suggestions from other students.

3. Discuss the following concepts:
    *   Why are we building rectangular prisms?
    *   What is the difference between a two-dimensional and three-dimensional object?
    *   What would it be like to be inside the box?
    *   What would it be like to be above or below the box?
    *   Which do you prefer and why?

Closure: Show the class an example of a pyramid, pointing out its base and sides. Have students complete the final activity: writing directions for building their own pyramid. After discussing what makes a good set of directions with your class, allow students to work in groups or alone to create the directions. Have the students exchange directions with each other and try them out, using paper to fold the pyramids. Revise or create a class set of directions for creating a pyramid.

Assessment: Teacher will evaluate the student's work using the Lesson 1 Rubric.

Independent Activities/Lesson Extension/Adaptations:

*   Geoboards: Using rubber bands and the geoboard, challenge the students to create as many right angles as possible. Vary the number of rubber bands used. Encourage students to create a horse for the knights of old or create a crown for a king.
*   Tangrams: Using the seven tans of a tangram, build a structure that will hold a small film canister of water. Water was difficult to transport in medieval times.
*   Students should be encouraged to make more boxes for inside and outside the castle by changing the dimensions.

lesson 1
story problems

Story Problem 1:

A wealthy landowner built a barn with the dimensions of 30 feet by 40 feet. What is the perimeter of his barn? What is the area of the floor of the barn?

   a) Perimeter = _____feet

   b) Area = _____square feet

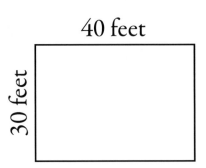

40 feet

30 feet

Story Problem 2:

The peasants are plowing the fields in preparation for planting the wheat. The furrows they are plowing are 100 feet long and 5 feet wide. There will be 50 rows total. How many total feet of plowing will be needed?

_____feet

lesson 1
make your castle box

corners

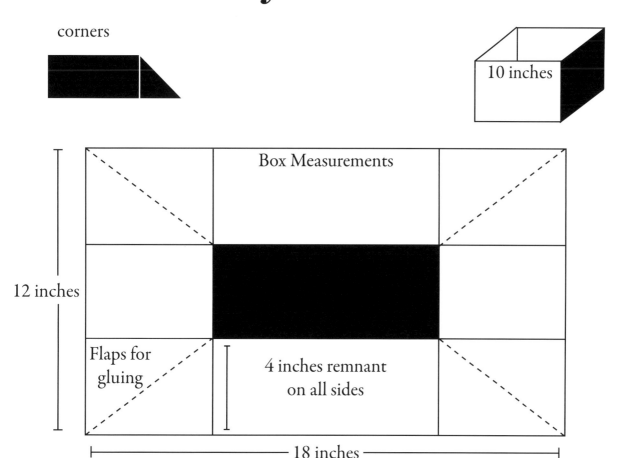

10 inches

Box Measurements

12 inches

Flaps for gluing

4 inches remnant on all sides

18 inches

---

directions:

1. Use a ruler to measure and place dots 4 inches toward the center of the box.
2. Connect all the dots.
3. Draw a diagonal dotted line at the corners as shown.
4. Fold on the heavy lines.
5. Cut, fold, and then glue the flaps together to make a box.
6. Glue the flaps down.
7. Secure the flaps with a paper clip.

lesson 1
writing activity

Directions:
Write a set of directions telling another person how to build a pyramid (another three-dimensional figure). You may only use 10 different direction statements and the picture. Once your directions are written, hand them to another student or your teacher and see if he or she can construct one.

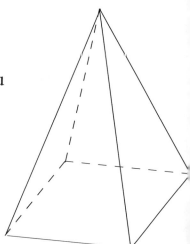

Materials you can use:
Pencil, Sheet of notebook paper, Scissors, Tape, Ruler

Your directions:

1. _____

_____

_____

2. _____

_____

_____

3. _____

_____

_____

4. _____

_____

lesson 1
writing activity, continued

5. _____

_____

_____

6. _____

_____

_____

7. _____

_____

_____

8. _____

_____

_____

9. _____

_____

_____

10. _____

_____

_____

Lesson 1 Rubric

	Below Expectations	Meets Expectations	Exceeds Expectations
Story Problem	Incorrect	Incorrect, but applied math correctly	Correct
Castle Box	Didn't follow directions; didn't complete box	Followed directions, but box is not sturdy; no right angles or incorrect perimeter	Followed directions; box is sturdy; right angles and perimeter are correct
Pyramid Directions	Did not write any directions; directions incorrect or unclear	Wrote correct directions	Correct, clear, and creative directions

Lesson 2
Sir Chip Square

Grade Level: 2–4

Approximate Length of Time: 2–3 hours

Prerequisite Knowledge:

- Historical information regarding castles
- Information about how castles are constructed
- Terms for review: right angle, square, outside lower level, narrative writing, perimeter, face side, cube
- Knowledge of how to measure the perimeter and area of a square

Rationale: Students research elements of a medieval castle using Internet resources. The teacher will assess the students' understanding of geometric principles using the pretest, and review any necessary principles. Students use their creativity to create a square character to add to their castle. Students use concepts related to squares to add a row of squares to the foundation of their castle.

National Standards Addressed:

- The student independently reads with fluency and understanding in texts at appropriate difficulty levels.
- The student selects and uses appropriate units and procedures to measure length and area.
- The student identifies and describes lines, shapes, and solids.
- The student applies measurement concepts to solve problems connected to everyday experiences.
- The student selects and uses writing processes in various forms.
- The student inquires and conducts research using a variety of sources.
- The student selects and uses writing processes for self-initiated and assigned writing.

Objectives: Students will be able to

- research castles using Internet resources;
- review and comprehend geometry principles through the pretest and ensuing discussion;
- create Sir Chip Square using concepts of a square;
- write a narrative about their square characters; and
- cut, color, and glue squares to the lower portion of their castle box.

Materials:

- worksheets for Lesson #2 (2 copies of Sir Chip Square master per student)
- copies of pretest for each student
- castle boxes from the previous lesson

- rulers, scissors, glue, construction paper, art materials, pencils
- Terms to Review handout

Procedure:

Opening Review: In a class discussion, discuss geometric terms from the Terms to Review handout. Pay special attention to the terms that apply to the geometric shape of a square. Brainstorm a list of three-dimensional objects that use the basic square.

Motivational or Introductory Approach: Prior to class, set up bookmarks on computers that deal with castles. "Castles have long been a part of history as a source of defense and protection. Today, we will research information with regard to castle history and construction. As you read and work on the selected sites, circle or underline any common information you find on the castle worksheet." Have students underline information they discover on their castle worksheet. Discuss the information students found as a class.

Development of Lesson:

1. After the class discussion, distribute the Geometric Principles pretest.
2. After the test, the answers should be discussed, so that all students have the opportunity to comprehend the geometric definitions.
3. Have students complete the story problems featuring Sir Chip Square.
4. Distribute construction paper and supplies for students to create a Sir Chip Square character of their own to add to their castle, following the instructions on their Lesson 2 worksheet.
5. Once the Sir Chip characters have been created, instruct the students to write a narrative paragraph about their character and his life in the castle. Be sure to remind them to answer the following questions in their narrative:
   - Why is he square?
   - What is his job?
   - Why might being a square make life difficult?
   - How does he get around?
   - If he is a chip off the old block, what happened to the old block?

Closure: Have students determine how many squares would be needed to cover the lower section of the castle box, measuring the perimeter of the box to do so. Students then color, cut, and paste the squares evenly around the lower half of the box. Students should be encouraged to texture or decorate their squares as they wish.

Assessment: Teacher will evaluate students using the Lesson 2 Rubric.

Independent Activities/Lesson Extension/Adaptations:

- Create a horse for Sir Chip using materials found in the classroom.
- Create a workable drawbridge for the castle.

lesson 2
the elements of a castle

"Once upon a time, a princess lived in a castle . . ." Many fairy tales begin this way. Castles were very real and important in the medieval period. In the Middle Ages, Europe was broken up into small regions that were controlled by the royal family and the nobility class, who were very rich people who owned land and helped the king and queen control their land and townspeople. Many castles were built on mountains. In times of war, the people of the town could go into the castle grounds for protection. The townspeople gave food and money to the lord of the castle in return for safety.

The first castles were surrounded by stout timber walls and later, castles were surrounded by thick stone or brick. The wall was topped by a walkway. Thick stonewalls jutted out from the lower wall with slits for shooting arrows or even throwing rocks. A moat sometimes surrounded the thick outer wall and could be filled with water. Some moats were dry, but had steep sides.

Drawbridges that could be pulled up at any time protected gates into the castle. Inside the walls was a large open courtyard called a ward. Store rooms, stables, barns, barracks, houses, and churches usually filled the ward. The headquarters of the king or lordship was in the ward in a fortified tower called a keep (in England) or a donjon (in France). Our word *dungeon* comes from the prisons that were located there.

Castles were generally uncomfortable places where safety was preferred over luxury. Most were cold, damp, and drafty.

geometric principles

Directions: Circle the correct answer.

1. A perimeter is:
a) the distance through an object
b) the distance around an object
c) the height of an object
d) none of the above

2. A face of a three-dimensional object is:
a) a large area
b) a plane surface bound by lines
c) a block
d) an angle

3. A side of a three-dimensional object is:
a) a corner where two line segments meet
b) a math operation to determine an answer
c) a length of line
d) a surface of an object next to the top and/or bottom

4. A cube is:
a) a solid having six equal sides or faces
b) a long line of solid shapes
c) a post with angles
d) an object with no corners

Round all the following answers to the nearest inch.

5. The perimeter of square A is_____ inches.

What is the perimeter of your box ?_____ inches

geometric principles, continued

6. Color the perimeter of square A red.

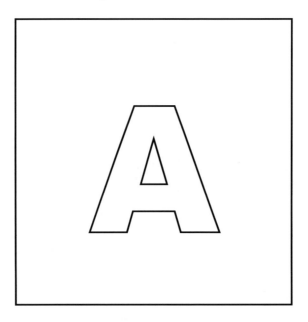

7. On the cube, figure B, color the top face blue.

8. Color the sides of the cube yellow.

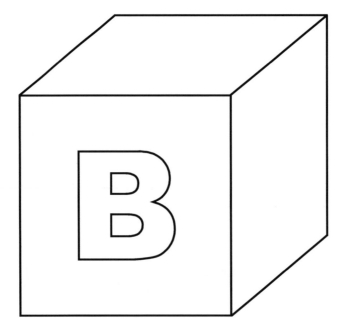

lesson 2
sir chip square's adventure

Story Problem 1:

Sir Chip Square is on a quest to capture a dragon from the depths of Lake Eviltar. Sir Chip must travel to several locations to gather the supplies he needs to capture the dragon. Measure the route he must take, starting at his home. How many total miles will he travel once he gathers all of the supplies and returns home?

Scale: 2 cm = 5 miles

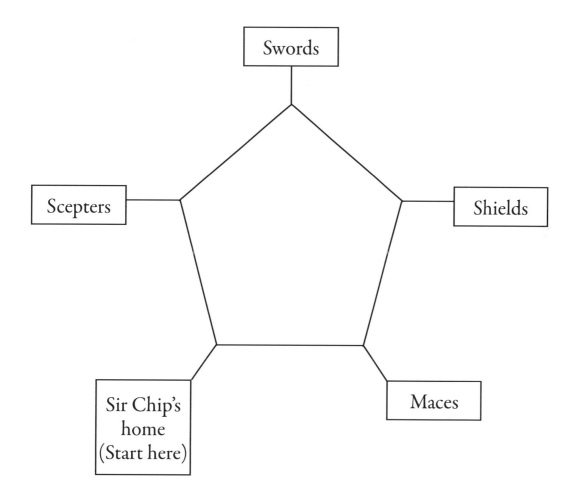

Total miles traveled: _____ miles

lesson 2
sir chip square's adventure continues

Story Problem 2:

Sir Chip Square collected all of the equipment he needed to capture the dragon. However, now he has to carry it a long distance, and the equipment and weapons are heavy. How much total weight must he carry?

16 ounces (oz) = 1 pound (lb)

Swords	12 lbs.	5 oz.
Shields	6 lbs.	2 oz.
Scepters	7 lbs.	9 oz.
Maces	9 lbs.	6 oz.

Answer = _____ lbs. _____ oz.

lesson 2
let's make sir chip square

Measure and cut a square from construction paper that is 5 inches long on all sides.
Add arms, legs, armor, and a sword to Sir Chip Square.

Tell Sir Chip Square's Story

Write a paragraph about Sir Chip. Be sure and answer the following questions about Sir Chip in your story. Why is he square and how did he get that way? What is his job? How does he get around? If he is a "chip off the old block," what happened to the old block? Is life difficult being a square? Why or why not?

Sir Chip's Tale

_____

_____

_____

_____

_____

_____

_____

_____

_____

_____

_____

castle bricks: sir chip square

1) Color and cut out the squares from the patterns below. These are square bricks.
2) Glue one row of squares to the lower half of the sides of your box. Do not glue them to the bottom face of the box. How many squares do you think you will need to cover the entire box? The squares are 2" x 2". Measure the perimeter of your box to determine how many squares you will need. The top of the box should be open.

Lesson 2 Rubric

	Below Expectations	Meets Expectations	Exceeds Expectations
Castle Research	Participated in research	Completed research and underlined similar facts	Completed research, underlined similar facts, and discussed findings
Pretest	1–3 correct answers	4–6 correct answers	7–8 correct answers
Sir Chip	Made Sir Chip	Followed directions for precise measurements	Followed directions, precise measurements, added original designs
Sir Chip's Tale	Wrote story about Chip, but didn't answer prompt questions	Wrote story about Chip answering prompt questions	Wrote original, creative, and grammatically correct story; answered prompt questions

Lesson 3
Princess Wreck Tangle

Grade Level: 2–4

Approximate Length of Time: 2–3 hours

Prerequisite Knowledge:

- Familiarity with rectangles and dominoes
- Terms for review: rectangle, right angle, outside upper lever, perimeter, face, rectangular prism, side, dominoes
- Knowledge of how to measure perimeter and area of a rectangle.

Rationale: Students will use higher level thinking to create a domino game and write the rules. A row of rectangles will be added to the outside upper level of their castle.

National Standards Addressed:

- The student selects and uses appropriate units and procedures to measure length and area.
- The student applies measurement concepts to solve problems connected to everyday experiences.
- The student selects and uses writing processes in various forms.
- The student inquires and conducts research using a variety of sources.

Objectives: Students will be able to:

- compute the perimeter and area of a rectangle;
- explore the topic of dominoes on the Internet;
- take notes of attributes to use or not use in their own games;
- create a set of dominoes and a domino game;
- write the directions for their domino game; and
- cut, color, and glue rectangles vertically above the squares.

Materials:

- worksheets for Lesson #3
- castle boxes from the previous lesson
- rulers, scissors, glue, construction paper, art materials, pencils
- Terms for Review handout

Procedure:

Opening Review: In a class discussion, discuss geometric terms from the Terms for Review handout. Pay special attention to the terms that apply to the geometric shape of a rectangle. Brainstorm a list of three-dimensional objects that use the basic rectangle. Discuss and complete the story problem for Lesson 3 as a class or individually.

Motivation or Introductory Approach: "Today, we will create a domino game using rectangles. We will also fortify your castles by adding rectangular bricks." Set up Web site bookmarks on computers that deal with dominoes (one good Web site is http://games.yahoo.com/games/rules/dominoes/gameplay.html). Allow students to visit Web sites about dominoes. As they interact with their Web sites, students should write down a few things about dominoes and rules they wish to incorporate in their own game later.

Development of Lesson:

1. Provide each student with a copy of the Castle Bricks worksheet. Instruct the students, "Because you have a time limit, keep your game simple, but creative." The students may work in groups if you wish.

2. Instruct students to address the following ideas when creating their games:
   - How many can play your game?
   - Who should start?
   - How do you win and count points? Is the high or low scorer the winner?
   - Do all dominoes have to have numbers on them?
   - What can be substituted for numbers?
   - Could the game have another use besides entertainment?

3. Given a time limit, permit the students to create the domino games. When the preset time is up, allow students to discuss and play the games.

Closure: Have students determine how many rectangles would be needed to cover the upper section of the castle box vertically above the squares using concepts of measurement. Students color, cut, and paste the rectangles evenly around the upper half of the box. Give students three copies of the Castle Bricks worksheet.

Assessment: Teacher will evaluate students using the Lesson 3 Rubric.

Independent Activities/Lesson Extension/Adaptations:

- Create a board game using shape characters.
- Create Princess Wreck Tangle to compliment Sir Chip and write a story about her life.
- Create thrones from shapes for the castle.

lesson 3
princess wreck tangle

Directions:

Answer the following questions.

2"

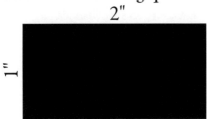

1"

Princess Wreck Tangle is adding bricks to the fortress. Her brick dimensions are 1" x 2".

Story Problem:

Princess Wreck Tangle needs to know how many rectangles she will need to go around her castle. Work the problems below to help her.

1. Measure the perimeter of your castle. Show your work.
    _____+_____+_____+_____=_____ inches
2. Estimate the number of bricks you will need if you place them vertically above the squares. I will need _____ bricks.
3. How many rows of brick will it take to reach the top? _____ row(s)
4. Color and decorate the rectangles creatively.
5. Cut out the rectangles. How many rectangles did you actually use? _____
6. What was the difference between your estimate and the number of bricks used? _____ bricks
7. Cover the upper portion of your castle in a row of rectangles above the squares.
8. Place the rectangles vertically.

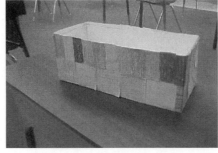

Your castle should look similar to this at this point.

lesson 3
domino game

Follow the directions:

Make a set of flat dominoes using the rectangle pattern your teacher has given you. A domino is a rectangular prism, a three-dimensional rectangle. Consider using another symbol besides dots for each domino. For example, your double one domino could look like this:

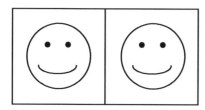

You will need to make 28 dominoes as listed below. Remember not to duplicate a domino.

Double blank, one/blank, two/blank, three/blank, four/blank, five/blank, six/blank

Double one, one/two, one/three, one/four, one/five, one/six

Double two, two/three, two/four, two/five, two/six

Double three, three/four, three/five, three/six

Double four, four/five, four/six

Double five, five/six

Double six

lesson 3
writing activity

Write a set of directions and rules for your domino game.

Name of the game:

Objective of the game (How do you win?):

Number of players:

Who starts:

Rules: _____

_____

_____

_____

_____

_____

_____

_____

_____

_____

_____

_____

Play a game with a classmate and/or your teacher. Change and refine your rules as needed.

 New York, NY: Routledge Copyright ©2006 Units of Instruction for Gifted Learners, Taylor & Francis. This page may be photocopied or reproduced with permission for students

castle bricks: princess wreck tangle

1. Color and cut out the rectangles from the patterns below. Make them look like rectangular bricks.
2. Glue one row of squares to the upper half of the sides of your box. How many rectangles do you think you will need? The rectangles are 2" x 1". The perimeter is 28".

Lesson 3 Rubric

	Below Expectations	Meets Expectations	Exceeds Expectations
Story Problem	1–3 correct	4–6 correct	7–8 correct
Domino Research	Participated in research	Participated and took notes about research	Participated, took notes, and applied research
Domino Game/ Directions	Did not write any directions; game unoriginal or hard to play	Wrote directions; game easy to play	Correct and clear directions; game original and easy to play

Lesson 4
The Knights of the Knagles

Grade Level: 2–4

Approximate Length of Time: 2–3 hours

Prerequisite Knowledge:

- Familiarity with triangles
- Terms for review: angles, right angle, obtuse angle, acute angle, scalene, isosceles, equilateral, perimeter
- Knowledge of perimeter and area of a triangle
- Knowledge of medieval family flags and crests

Rationale: Students create flags or pennants of various triangular properties to add on the four corners of their castle product. Students will create symbols for their flags and write explanations of their chosen symbols.

National Standards Addressed:

- The student selects and uses writing processes in various forms.
- The student inquires and conducts research using a variety of sources.
- The student selects and uses appropriate units and procedures to measure length and area.
- The student selects and uses writing processes for self-initiated and assigned writing.
- The student uses geometric vocabulary to describe angles. The student is expected to:
    - use angle measurements to classify angles as acute, obtuse, or right; and
    - identify relationships involving angles in triangles and quadrilaterals.

Objectives: Students will be able to:

- compute the perimeter and area of triangles;
- explore the topic of medieval flags and family crests on the Internet and take notes;
- create flags;
- explain the symbols they chose for their flags; and
- cut, color, and glue flags on the corners of their castle.

Materials:

- worksheets for Lesson #4
- castle boxes from the previous lesson
- pencils, notebook paper, toothpicks, rulers, scissors, glue, construction paper
- other art supplies as needed
- Terms for Review handout

Procedure:

Opening Review: In a class discussion, discuss geometric terms from the Terms for Review handout. Pay special attention to the terms that apply to the geometric shape of a triangle. Brainstorm a list of three-dimensional objects that use the basic triangle and discuss.

Motivation or Introductory Approach: "Today, we will elaborate our castle with triangle flags and pennants. These will be placed on the corners of your castle box. You will need to add meaningful symbols and explain their meaning." Set up Web site bookmarks on computers that deal with medieval flags and family crests. Allow students to go to bookmarked Web sites and research medieval flags and family crests. As they interact with the Web sites, students should write down a few attributes of flags and crests. Students may also practice drawing some of the items they like on their paper.

Development of Lesson:

1. Discuss and complete the story problem for Lesson 4 as a class or individually.
2. Distribute the triangle samples. Instruct the students, "Select the triangle shapes you wish to use. Make a list of the symbols you would like to use."
3. Discuss the following ideas as a class:
   - Because many people could not read during medieval times, why were symbols so important?
   - What is the importance of the color of many symbols?
   - What is the difference of flags today and then?
   - What is a family crest?
   - What do flags tell of family heritage?
   - What symbols can be combined?
   - What symbols can be adapted or modified?
   - What purpose do flags, symbols, and crests serve?
4. Once the flags are finished, have the students present and discuss their creations and write their symbol interpretations and explanations.

Closure: Students color, cut, and paste the flags on the corners.

Assessment: Teachers will evaluate students using the Lesson 4 Rubric.

Independent Activities/Lesson Extension/Adaptations:

- Create a personal family shield.
- Create an original modern day symbol to represent something of importance to the student.
- Research family trees and histories, and have each student prepare his or her own family tree to share with the class.

lesson 4
the knights of the knagles

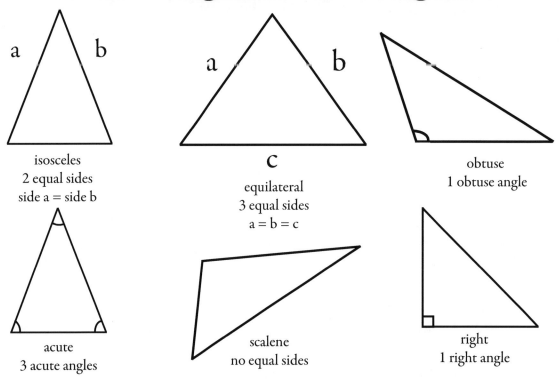

isosceles
2 equal sides
side a = side b

equilateral
3 equal sides
a = b = c

obtuse
1 obtuse angle

acute
3 acute angles

scalene
no equal sides

right
1 right angle

Knights were professional soldiers. Most knights traveled looking for work. In the 12th century, French tournaments were an essential part of military and social life. The knights used lances or swords that were not sharp, but blunted, in their jousts, or games.

Terms for Review:

Right Angle: a 90 degree angle formed by two perpendicular lines.

Obtuse Angle: an angle greater than 90 degrees, but less than 180 degrees.

Acute Angle: an angle of less than 90 degrees.

Scalene Triangle: a triangle where no sides have the same lengths.

Isosceles Triangle: a triangle where two sides have the same lengths.

Equilateral Triangle: a triangle where all sides have the same lengths.

story problem

Directions:

The knights had to travel around the triangles below. Measure the perimeter of all the triangles below to the nearest inch. Add up the segments. What is the total length of all the segments you measured?

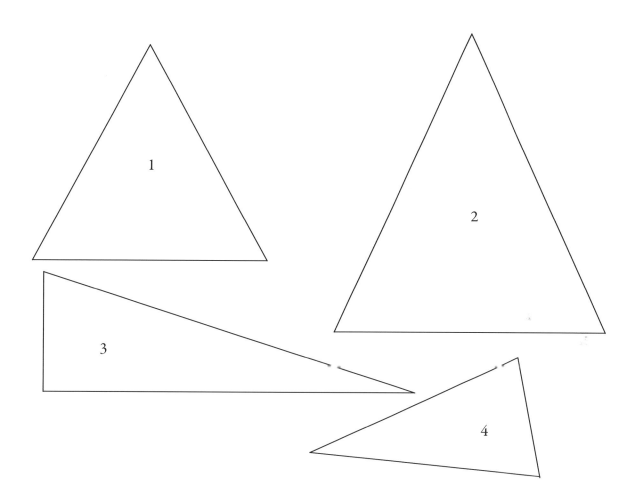

Round all your measurements to the nearest inch.

Triangle #1 _____   Triangle #3 _____

Triangle #2 _____   Triangle #4 _____

Total length of all segments = _____ inches

lesson 4
flag pattern page

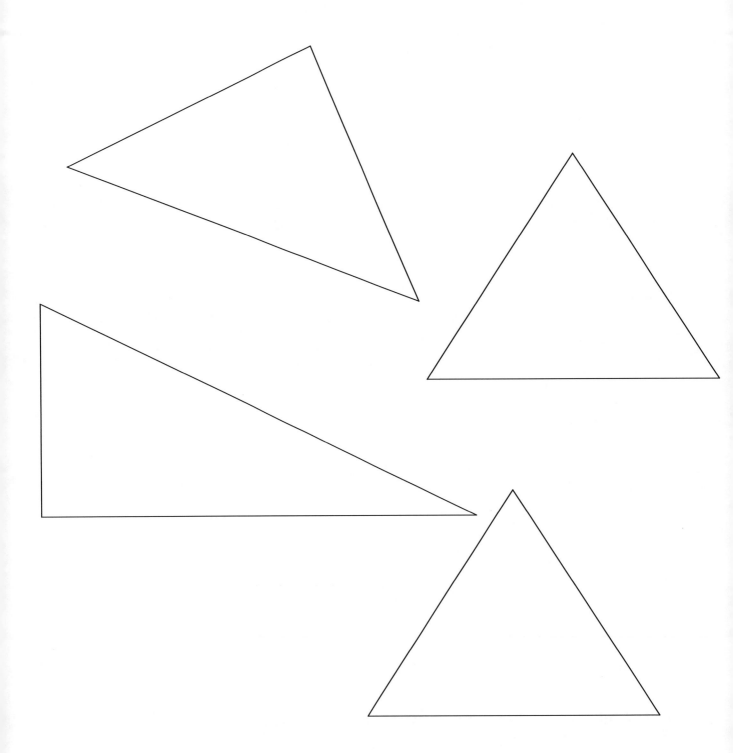

lesson 4
flag pattern page, continued

Directions:

1. Cut out all of the triangular shapes from the Flag Pattern Page and create flags for your castle. Roll up paper or use toothpicks to create a staff or pole for your flag.

2. Add symbols to represent your castle. Create four different symbols. For example, you might want to include an animal to represent your family, horses or boats to represent the way you travel, or stripes and other shapes for decoration.

3. Use tape to add the flags to the four corners of your castle.

List the symbols you created and explain what they represent:

1.

2.

3.

4.

Lesson 4 Rubric

	Below Expectations	Meets Expectations	Exceeds Expectations
Flag	Participated in research	Participated and took notes	Participated, took notes, and applied research
Symbols Discussion of Prior Research	Did not participate	Participated in discussion	Participated and showed understanding
Flag/ Symbols Creation	Created flags and symbols	Created flags and symbols; showed originality	Created flags and symbols with original designs and applied facts from research

Lesson 5
The Holies and the Not-So-Holies

Grade Level: 2–4

Approximate Length of Time: 2–3 hours

Prerequisite Knowledge:

- Terms for review: circle, oval, pentagon, hexagon, octagon, perimeter, compass
- Information about shields and swords
- Knowledge pertaining to circles, hexagons, octagons, ovals, and pentagons

Rationale: Students will design and add a sword and shield to their castle. Students will use compasses to draw circles and create a flower for the outside of their castle.

National Standards Addressed:

- The student applies measurement concepts to solve problems connected to everyday experiences.
- The student selects and uses writing processes in various forms.
- The student selects and uses writing processes for self-initiated and assigned writing.

Objectives: Students will be able to:

- solve a story problem;
- color, cut, and arrange shapes to create a sword and shield;
- use a compass to create a flower with precise measurements; and
- write a diamante poem.

Materials:

- worksheets for Lesson #5
- castle boxes from the previous lesson
- pencils, scissors, glue or glue sticks, construction paper, art supplies
- Terms for Review handout
- compasses
- a small piece of clay for each student
- pipe cleaners: about 6 inches in length

Procedure:

Opening Review: In a class discussion, discuss geometric terms from the Terms for Review handout. Pay special attention to the terms that apply to the geometric shape of a circle, oval, hexagon, octagon, and pentagon. Brainstorm a list of three-dimensional objects that use these shapes and discuss.

Motivation or Introductory Approach: "Today, we will add some decorations to our castle. These will be placed where you like on or around the castle. You can make other decorations as your creativity demands." Discuss and complete the story problem individually or as a class.

Development of Lesson:

1. Explain to the students, "Now you are going to make a sword and shield using circle and octagonal shapes. You will need to cut out the pieces and recreate the design as shown."

2. Once the sword and shield is complete, teachers should instruct their students to create compass flowers. "Next, you are to make flowers to decorate the castle grounds. To begin, use a compass. Draw 6 or 7 circles with 2-inch diameters on your choice of colored construction paper."

3. Allow student to create flowers and elaborate.

4. Discuss and ask the students to brainstorm what might be around a castle. Some discussion questions might be:
   - If you were standing on the top of the castle, what might you see?
   - What would the people be doing in and around the castle?
   - How do people get water, food, and clothes?
   - What differences would you see from what you see today?
   - How would the serfs make their fences?
   - What kind of farming would you see?

5. Once the shield and flowers are created, have the students write a diamante poem on the flower pattern. The flower can be used to decorate the grounds of the castle. Distribute the diamante writing directions to each student.

6. Have students complete the chart, using a thesaurus or dictionary if needed.

7. Using the words from the chart, ask the students to compose a diamante poem about common 3-D objects. The top half of the poem is dedicated to one shape with straight lines (boxes, homes, gifts). The bottom half is dedicated to curved edges like an oval or circle (sun, ball, football).

Closure: Have the students rewrite their poem on the pattern. Attach the poem to a pipe cleaner and place on the castle grounds.

Assessment: Teacher will evaluate students using the Lesson 5 Rubric.

lesson 5
the holies and the not-so-holies

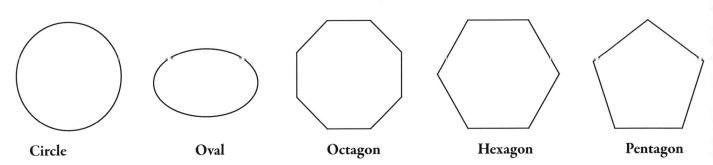

Circle   Oval   Octagon   Hexagon   Pentagon

Story Problem:
Complete the math and fill in the blanks.

 The Not-So Holies (Octagon, Hexagon, and Pentagon) went to the
Holies (Circle and Oval) for confession and to pay taxes to the Lord
of the Land. The taxes were being paid for protection of the knights.
Octagon paid 8 pounds, Hexagon paid 6 pounds, and Pentagon paid
5 pounds. Altogether they paid _____ pounds.

The Lords With No Edges kept 7 pounds for themselves. The Lord
of the Land then received _____ pounds. The Lord's Lady took
half of that, which then left the Lord of the Land _____ pounds.
Grain for his livestock cost 6 pounds. How much did the Lord of the
Land have left? _____ pounds.

lesson 5
the sword and the shield

- Directions: Cut out the shapes below.
- Color, arrange, and glue together the sword and shield.

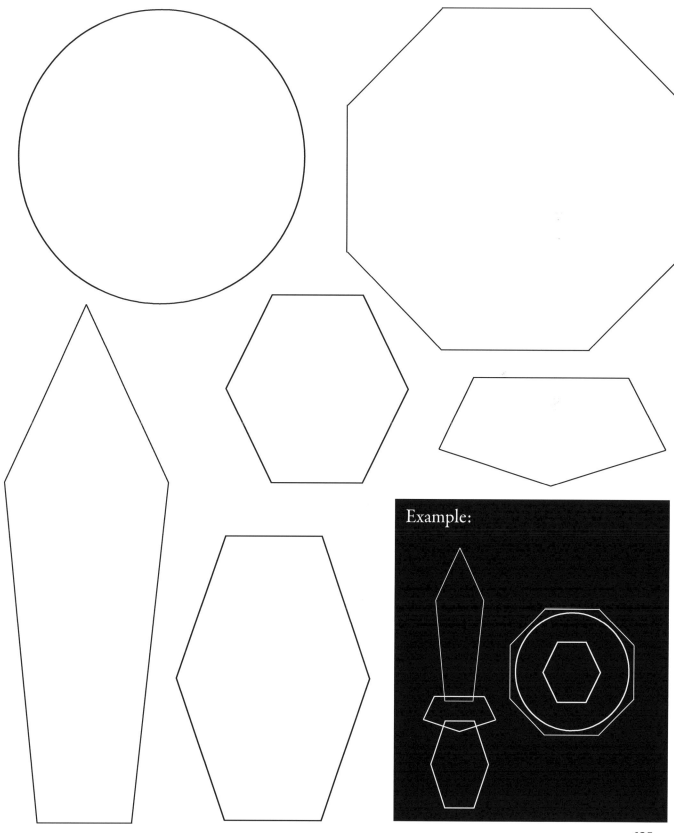

Example:

lesson 5
make a compass flower

Materials:

- Colored construction paper
- Compass
- Pencil
- Glue or glue sticks
- A small piece of clay
- Pipe cleaners: about 6 inches in length

Directions:

1. Using a compass, draw 6 or 7 circles with 2-inch diameters on your choice of colored construction paper.
2. Cut out the circles and glue them around a center circle.
3. Allow the flower time to dry.
4. Glue or tape the flower to a pipe cleaner. Use a scrap of paper and glue the pipe cleaner to the back of the flower.
5. Stick the pipe cleaner in a mound of clay. Place the flower in or around the castle.

lesson 5
diamante poem

Complete the chart. Use a thesaurus or dictionary and brainstorm. Using the words from the chart, compose a diamante poem, following the guidelines on the next page.

3-D Objects With Straight Lines

Name 3 objects with straight lines:

_____ _____ _____

Adjectives: Descriptions

_____ _____ _____

_____ _____ _____

Verbs (-ing words)

_____ _____ _____

_____ _____ _____

3-D Objects With Curved Lines

Name 3 objects with curved lines

_____ _____ _____

Adjectives: Descriptions

_____ _____ _____

_____ _____ _____

Verbs (-ing words)

_____ _____ _____

_____ _____ _____

diamante

The top half of the poem is dedicated to one shape.
The bottom half is dedicated to another shape.

_____

(Object)

_____ _____

(Pick two adjectives about the above object)

_____ _____ _____

(Pick three -ing words about the object above)

_____ _____   _____ _____

(Two nouns about the shaped object at the top)   (Two nouns about the shaped object at the bottom)

_____ _____ _____

(Pick three -ing words about the object below)

_____ _____

(Pick two adjectives about the object below)

_____

(Pick the opposite shape)

me_____   Date_____

Rewrite your poem on the following pattern.

Lesson 5 Rubric

	Below Expectations	Meets Expectations	Exceeds Expectations
Story Problem	Incorrect	Incorrect, but applied math correctly	Correct
Sword, Shield, Compass Flower	Made sword, shield, and compass flower	Made sword, shield, and compass flower; neat construction	Made sword, shield, and compass flower; neat construction; added original design elements
Diamante Poem	Filled in chart; wrote a poem on flower pattern	Filled in chart; wrote poem demonstrating an understanding of geometric principles	Filled in chart; listed other ideas; wrote poem demonstrating an understanding of geometric principles; showed creativity and originality

Terms for Review

1. *Acute Angle:* an angle of less than 90 degrees
2. *Area:* the surface or inside the perimeter; formula = L x W
3. *Compass:* a device used for drawing circles and arcs
4. *Cube:* A cube has six surfaces and twelve edges of equal length.
5. *Equilateral Triangle*: a triangle where all sides have the same lengths
6. *Face of a three-dimensional object:* a wall or surface on a geometric solid
7. *Hexagon:* a plane figure having six angles and six sides
8. *Isosceles Triangle:* a triangle where two sides have the same lengths
9. *Line Segment:* the part of a line between two points
10. *Obtuse Angle:* an angle greater than 90 degrees, but less than 180 degrees
11. *Octagon*: a plane geometric figure bounded by eight line segments with eight angles
12. *Oval:* resembling an egg or an ellipse in shape
13. *Pentagon:* a plane geometric figure bounded by five line segments and containing five angles
14. *Rectangular Prism:* a closed figure whose bases are rectangles and whose other faces are parallelograms
15. *Perpendicular lines*: lines that meet and form a corner of 90 degrees
16. *Perimeter:* the outer limits of an area; formula for a four sided figure = S1 + S2 + S3 + S4
17. *Right Angle:* a 90 degree angle formed by two perpendicular lines
18. *Scalene Triangle:* a triangle where no sides have the same lengths
19. *Side of a three-dimensional object*: the surface next to the top or bottom
20. *Two dimensions:* any two from width, depth, or length (for example, square and rectangle)
21. *Three dimensions:* width, length, and depth (for example, cube and prism)

Answer Key for Sir Faces

Lesson 1: Story Problem

1a. 140 feet

1b. 1,200 square feet

2. 25,000 feet

Lesson 2: Geometric Principles

1. b

2. b

3. d

4. a

5. 12 inches, 18 inches

Lesson 2: Story Problems:

1. 100 miles

2. 35 lbs., 6 oz.

Lesson 3:

1. _10_ + _10_ + _4_ + _4_ = _28_ inches

2. Answers will vary

3. _2_ row(s) of bricks are needed to reach the top

4. Rectangles will vary.

5. _18_

6. Answers will vary.

Lesson 4:

Measured to the nearest inch (.5 inches and greater will require the students to round upward).

Triangle #1 = 9 inches

Triangle #2 = 9 inches

Triangle #3 = 9 inches

Triangle #4 = 6 inches

Total Inches = 33 inches

Lesson 5: Story Problem

The Not-So Holies (Octagon, Hexagon, and Pentagon) went to the Holies (Circle and

Oval) for confession and to pay taxes to the Lord of the Land. The taxes were being paid for protection of the knights. Octagon paid 8 pounds, Hexagon paid 6 pounds and Pentagon paid 5 pounds. Altogether they paid __19__ pounds.

The Lords With No Edges kept 7 pounds for themselves. The Lord of the Land then kept the __12__ pounds remaining. The Lord's Lady took half of that which then left the Lord of the land __6__ pounds.

Grain for his livestock cost 6 pounds. How much did the Lord of the Land have left? __0__ pounds.

Independent Activities/Lesson Extension/Adaptations:

Choose one of these activities to complete as the end of unit activity:

- Devise a workable drawbridge for the castle. Write an explanation of how your drawbridge works. Include any simple machines used.
- Elaborate the castle grounds with creative three-dimensional figures. Write and perform a play with the castle grounds as a setting.
- Elaborate the castle interior with small buildings and people. Search the Web for castles and castle information for your elaboration ideas.
- Create a family shield and write a paragraph describing it in detail. Study the genealogy of your family tree and create a shield with symbols.
- Create cylinders to be used as castle towers on the corners. Paper trapezoids and squares can be rolled up and used as cylinders. Empty toilet paper rolls are handy, too.
- Read Rapunzel. Write you own fairy tale using the tower as the setting. Use Sir Chip Square, Princess Wreck Tangle, The Knights of the Knagles, and the Holies and Not-So-Holies in your tale, or be creative and think up your own characters.
- Create a moat. Write a story from the point of view of a frog living in the moat.

The Geometry Box Project

—Developed by Connie Simons

Unit Overview: Student interactions with volume and area begin at the concrete level as they guess, estimate, and compute the surface area and volume of a collection of small boxes. Questioning provides opportunities for students to analyze findings and share information with peers. This unit is developed for small groups of mathematically talented students and is not designed to be graded.

Resources Needed:
- a folder for each student containing lesson sheets and answer key
- a selection of small, interesting boxes (such as check boxes, card boxes, candy boxes), at least one per student, but two or three per student is better
- square inches cut from pattern
- cubic inches cut from pattern and taped
- protractors or note cards to identify right angles
- calculator for each student
- scissors for each student
- tape

Helpful Resources:
- *Math at Hand: A Mathematics Handbook* by Great Source Education Group, 1999, ISBN# 0-66946-922-8
- *Developing Math Talent: A Guide for Teachers and Parents of Gifted Students* by Susan Assouline and Ann Lupkowski-Shoplik, 2005, ISBN# 1-59363-159-6
- *Math On Call: A Mathematics Handbook* by Andrew Kaplan, 2004, ISBN# 0-66950-819-5
- *Geometry: Cliffs Quick Review* by Ed Kohn, 2001, ISBN# 0-76456-380-7
- *Challenge Math* by Edward Zaccaro, 2005, ISBN# 0-96799-155-2

Lesson 1
Attributes of a Box

Grade Level: 4–5

Approximate Length of Time: 30 minutes

Prerequisite Knowledge:

- *Attributes* are unique properties or characteristics.

Rationale: By studying the attributes of a box, students will discover the attributes of a right rectangular prism.

National Standard Addressed: Students will analyze characteristics and properties of two- and three-dimensional shapes.

Objectives: Students will be able to:

- identify the number of faces of a box,
- identify the number of sets of parallel faces,
- identify the number of right angles on the surface of a box, and
- identify and label bases and lateral faces.

Materials:

- a collection of small rectangular boxes with lids (at least one per student—two or three per student is better)
- scissors for each student
- tape
- note cards (to use corner of card to find right angle of box) or small protractor

Procedure:

Opening: Hold up a small box and invite students to choose one of the boxes for examination. Tell students they will be studying the attributes, or unique characteristics that make the boxes *right rectangular prisms*. Have students examine the boxes and begin thinking about why they are right rectangular prisms. Students then record their observations under question 1 on their Lesson 1 worksheet, and share their responses with their peers.

Development of Lesson:

1. Emphasize that a box has equal parallel sides. The sides of a box are known as *faces*. Point out a set of parallel faces on your box and have students do the same with their boxes.

2. Use a corner of a note card or a small protractor to point out the three right angles on a corner of your box. Have the students do the same with a corner of their box. Have the students complete question 2 on their Lesson 1 worksheet and compare responses.

3. Place your box on a table and tell students the side of the box it is

resting on and its opposite side are called *bases*. Turn your box so that it rests on another side and demonstrate that a different side, or face, of the box is now the base.

4. The sides of the box are known as *lateral faces*. Lateral means *side*. Have students complete question 3 of their Lesson 1 worksheet by lightly taping *base* and *lateral face* labels on their boxes.

Closing: Hold up a box and ask students why it is a right rectangular prism. (It has equal parallel sides.)

Assessment: Assign one student to record responses as students answer the question, "After today's lesson, what do we know about right rectangular prisms?" Have students refer to the student sheet and answer key to verify their responses.

lesson 1
attributes of a box

Materials: a collection of small rectangular boxes with lids, scissors, tape

1. Examine the boxes. Why do you think these boxes are called *right rectangular prisms*? What features make them right rectangular prisms?

    Share your responses with the other group members.

2. Choose one of the boxes and answer the following questions.

    How many sides, or faces, does the box have? _____

    How many sets of parallel faces does the box have?
    _____

    How many right angles does the box have? _____

    Compare your responses to your group members' responses.

3. The faces on the top and bottom of the box are known as *bases*. The sides are known as *lateral faces*. Cut out the labels for bases and lateral faces and tape them to the box you chose. Remember that any side can be either a base or a lateral face, depending on which side the box is resting.

New York, NY: Routledge Copyright ©2006 Units of Instruction for Gifted Learners, Taylor & Francis. This page may be photocopied or reproduced with permission for stude

base

base

lateral face

lateral face

lateral face

lateral face

Lesson 2
Surface Area

Grade Level: 4–5

Approximate Length of Time: 30 minutes

Prerequisite Knowledge:

- Area is the interior measure of a flat figure.
- The area of a rectangle equals the measurement of the length times the measurement of the width.
- Area is measured in square units.

Rationale: Students will apply knowledge of area to the faces of a box, or right rectangular prism.

National Standard Addressed: Students will analyze characteristics and properties of two- and three-dimensional shapes.

Objectives: Students will be able to:

- write a paraphrased definition of area in 10 words or less;
- guess, estimate, and compute the area of the face of a box, or right rectangular prism; and
- use a calculator to compute area by rounding measurements to the nearest quarter-inch, converted to its decimal equivalent.

Materials:

- boxes
- square inches (cut from pattern)
- rulers
- calculators for each student

Procedure:

Opening: Ask students what they remember about area and have one student record the responses. Have students complete the paraphrase for definition of area on their Lesson 2 worksheet, and share responses.

Development of Lesson:

1. Hold up a box and ask students how many sides, or faces, the box has. Point out that each face has its own area that can be measured. Give each student a square inch and ask why it is called a square inch. Have students choose a box and one face of the box. Without picking up the square inch, have students guess how many square inches make up the area of the face they selected and record their guess under question 2 of their Lesson 2 worksheet.

2. Demonstrate moving a square inch across the face of the box to estimate how many square inches make up the area. Have students do the same with their boxes and record their answers on their worksheets.

3. Demonstrate measuring the face of your box and rounding the measurements to the nearest quarter inch. Have a student read the decimal conversions (¼ = .25, ½ = .5, ¾ = .75) provided on their Lesson 2 worksheet as you demonstrate computing length times width with a calculator to find the area. Ask students why you are labeling the area with square inches. Have students compute the area of the face of their boxes. Have students choose another box face that is not a parallel face, and guess, estimate, and compute its area. Students should record their responses under question 2 of their worksheets.

Closing/Assessment: Have students analyze their work for this lesson by completing question 3 on their student worksheets and sharing responses with their classmates.

Ask students what the *total surface area* of a right rectangular prism might be. How might we find it?

lesson 2
surface area

Materials: boxes, square inches (see pattern), rulers, calculators

1. Read the definition of area and then paraphrase it in your own words using 10 words or less.

Area is a measure of the interior of a planar (flat) figure. It is expressed in square units such as inches or centimeters.

Paraphrase of the definition in my own words:

_____

_____

_____

Share your response with your group members.

2. Choose one face of any box and place a square inch on the table next to it. Without touching either, guess how many square inches make up the area of the face. Record your guess below.

Pick up the square inch and move it across the face of the box to estimate the number of square inches. Record your estimate.

Compute the surface area of the face by multiplying the length of the face (how long it is) by the width (how wide it is). Measure to the nearest quarter inch and convert fractions to decimals (¼ = .25; ½ = .5; ¾ = .75).

Choose another face and repeat the steps above.

Face Area	Guess	Estimate	Actual (A = l x w)
Face #1	_____	_____	_____ square inches (in.)
Face #2	_____	_____	_____ square inches (in.)

3. Analyze:

   a. Did your guess and estimation match the actual area? _____
      Why or why not?

   _____

   _____

   _____

   b. Why is the area of a face labeled with square inches?

   _____

   _____

   _____

Share your responses with your group members.

4. Stretch:

   a. What is total surface area?

   _____

   _____

   _____

   b. How would we find it?

   _____

   _____

   _____

Share your response with your group members.

After you have completed your worksheet, compare you answers
with those on the answer key.

Name_____   **lesson 2**   Date_____
square inch pattern

New York, NY: Routledge Copyright ©2006 Units of Instruction for Gifted Learners, Taylor & Francis. This page may be photocopied or reproduced with permission for student

Lesson 3
Total Surface Area

Grade Level: 4–5

Approximate Length of Time: 30 minutes

Prerequisite Knowledge:

- area
- use of calculator to compute area (from Lesson 2)

Rationale: Students will extend knowledge of area to total surface area of a right rectangular prism.

National Standard Addressed: Students will analyze characteristics and properties of two- and three-dimensional shapes.

Objective: Students will be able to:

- compute the total surface area of a box, or right rectangular prism, by computing the area of the bases and lateral faces and adding the measurements together.

Materials:

- boxes
- rulers
- calculators for each student

Procedure:

Opening: Ask students how they found the area of the face of a box. Ask what they think the total surface area of a box would be, and how they would find it.

Development of Lesson:

1. Hold up a box and demonstrate that the box has six sides, each with its own area. We can find the total surface area by adding the area of the six sides.
2. Ask students how many sets of parallel faces the box has. Point out that the bases are parallel faces and will have the same area. Point out the two sets of lateral faces that will have the same area. Students will only have to compute the area for one of the faces for each parallel set, because the other face in the set will have an equal area. Have students complete question 1 on their Lesson 3 worksheet to compute the total surface area for a box they select.

Closing: Ask students how they could use what they have learned to compute the total surface area of the classroom door.

Assessment: Have students read the formula for finding the total surface area of a right rectangular prism and give a written explanation of why the formula works on question 2 of their worksheets. Have students choose another box and find the total surface area, recording their responses under question 3 of their worksheets.

Independent Activities/Lesson Extension/Adaptations:

Make a square foot and use it to estimate and compute the total surface area of the classroom door.

lesson 3
total surface area

Materials: boxes, rulers, calculators

1. Choose a box. Find the total surface area of the box by computing the area of the faces and bases and then adding all of the areas together.

   Base #1 _____ square inches (in.^{2})
   Base #2 _____ square inches (in.^{2})

   Parallel face #1 _____ square inches (in.^{2})
   Parallel face #2 _____ square inches (in.^{2})

   Parallel face #1 _____ square inches (in.^{2})
   Parallel face #2 _____ square inches (in.^{2})

   Total Surface Area _____ square inches (in.^{2})

   The formula for finding the total surface area of a right rectangular prism is:

   Total Surface Area = 2lw + 2lh + 2wh (2 length times width, plus 2 length times height, plus 2 width times height)

2. Why does this formula work? Write a response, and then share it with your group members.

_____

_____

_____

_____

3. Choose another box and find the total surface area using the formula.

2lw = _____ in.
2lh = _____ in.
2wh = _____ in.

Total Surface Area = _____ in. ^{2}

4. Stretch:

Make a square foot and use it to estimate the total surface area of the classroom door. Measure and compute the actual total surface area of the door.

Lesson 4
Volume

Grade Level: 4–5

Approximate Length of Time: 30–60 minutes

Prerequisite Knowledge:

- Volume is the measure of an interior of a solid, or the number of unit cubes necessary to fill a solid.
- Volume is found by multiplying the measurement of the length times the measurement of the width times the measurement of the height.

Rationale: Students will internalize the concept of volume as they manipulate boxes and cubic inches.

National Standard Addressed: Students will analyze characteristics and properties of two- and three-dimensional shapes.

Objectives: Students will be able to:

- write a paraphrased definition of volume in 10 words or less;
- guess, estimate and calculate the volume of a several boxes, or right rectangular prisms; and
- use a calculator to compute the volume of boxes by rounding measurements to the nearest quarter-inch, converted to the decimal equivalent.

Materials:

- boxes (randomly numbered with sticky notes)
- rulers and calculators for each student
- cubic inches for each student (cut from pattern and taped together)
- scissors
- tape

Procedure:

Opening: Ask students what they know about *volume*, the measure of an interior of a solid, and have one student record the responses. Hold up a box and remove the lid, putting a hand inside to show the interior of the box (i.e., the volume). If the box were filled with sand, for example, how much sand would it hold?

Development of Lesson:

1. Have students complete question 1 on their Lesson 4 worksheet, paraphrasing the definition of volume, then share their response with classmates.

2. Give students a cubic inch and have them select a box. Talk about why it is a cubic inch (i.e., it is three-dimensional with each side measuring 1 inch by 1 inch). Without putting the cubic inch inside the box, ask students to guess the box's volume by thinking about how many cubic

inches it will hold. Have students record their guess under question 2 of their worksheets.

3. Demonstrate estimating how many cubic inches the box will hold by placing the cubic inch in the box and moving it across the box. Have students do the same and record their estimate under question 2 of their worksheets.

4. Demonstrate measuring the length, width, and height of your box, rounding to the nearest quarter inch, and using a calculator to compute volume by multiplying length times width times height. Ask students why you will label the volume with cubic inches. Have the students repeat the process with their boxes and record the volume of their boxes under question 2 on their worksheets. Have students repeat the guessing, estimating, and computing of the volume of boxes with several different boxes, recording their information on their worksheets.

Closing: Have students compare the computed volumes for the volumes other students figured for the same boxes. Do they match? Are they close?

Assessment: Have students complete questions 3 and 4 on their worksheets and share responses.

Independent Activities/Lesson Extension/Adaptations:

Have students make a cubic foot and use it to guess, estimate, and compute the actual volume of the classroom. Have students use a meter stick to compute the actual volume of the classroom in meters. Have students make a cubic centimeter and guess, estimate, and compute the volume of one of the small boxes in cubic centimeters.

Materials: boxes (randomly numbered with sticky notes), rulers, calculators, cubic inches, scissors, tape

1. Read the definition of volume and then paraphrase it in your own words using 10 words or less.

Volume is a measure of the interior of a solid; the number of unit cubes necessary to fill the interior of a solid.

Paraphrase of the definition in my own words:

_____

_____

_____

Share your response with your group members.

2. Select a box and set a cubic inch beside it on the table. Without touching either, guess how many cubic inches are in the box. Record your guess.

Pick up the cubic inch and the box. Place the cubic inch inside the box and estimate how many cubic inches are in the box. Record the estimate.

The formula for finding the volume of a right rectangular prism is V = l x w x h (Volume = length x width x height).

Use a ruler to measure the length, width, and height of the box to the nearest quarter inch. Convert fractions to decimals and use a calculator to compute the actual volume. Label with cubic inches (in.³).

Follow the same procedures with different boxes and record the data in the chart on the next page.

Volume of a Box

	Guess	Estimate	Actual ($V = l \times w \times h$)
Box # ____	____ in.	____ in.	____ in.^{3}
Box # ____	____ in.	____ in.	____ in.^{3}
Box # ____	____ in.	____ in.	____ in.^{3}
Box # ____	____ in.	____ in.	____ in.^{3}
Box # ____	____ in.	____ in.	____ in.^{3}

3. Analyze:

a. Compare actual volumes for the numbered boxes with your group members. Are they close to the volume others got for the same boxes?

_____

_____

_____

b. Did the guesses and estimations with cubic inches match the actual volume?

_____

_____

_____

c. Why or why not?

_____

_____

_____

d. What patterns do you notice in the guesses and estimations?

_____

_____

_____

e. What might cause us to make mistakes when computing volume?

_____

_____

_____

Share your responses with your group members.

4. Stretch:

a. Why does V = l x w x h work when computing volume?

_____

_____

_____

b. Why are two measurements multiplied for area and three measurements multiplied for volume?

_____

_____

_____

5. Stretch:

- Make a cubic foot and use it to estimate the volume of larger boxes. Compute the actual volume in cubic feet.
- Use a meter stick to compute the volume of the classroom in cubic meters.
- Make a cubic centimeter and guess, estimate, and compute the volume of one of the small boxes in cubic centimeters.

lesson 4
cubic inch pattern

Date_____

Lesson 5
Make a Talking Box

Grade Level: 4–5

Approximate Length of Time: 30 minutes

Prerequisite Knowledge:

- Definitions of *base*, *lateral face*, *right angle*, *total surface area*, and *volume* from previous lessons

Rationale: Students will summarize unit learning by building a box (made from the pattern included at the end of this unit) and recording information about the box's dimensions on its faces.

National Standard Addressed: Students will analyze characteristics of and properties of two- and three-dimensional shapes.

Objectives: Students will be able to:

- identify the number of bases on a box,
- identify the number of lateral faces on a box,
- identify the number of right angles on a box,
- determine the total surface area of a box, and
- compute the volume of a box.

Materials:

- Talking Box pattern
- tape
- ruler, calculator, and scissors for each student

Procedure:

Opening: Show the Talking Box pattern and demonstrate cutting it out and folding to make a box, but do not tape it together. Unfold the box and point out to students that they will be putting information on the faces of the box that will show when it is taped together. Tell students the Talking Box will include information they have learned in the Geometry Box Project as they studied right rectangular prisms.
Development of the Lesson:
1. Have students follow the steps listed on their Talking Box directions sheet. Encourage them to refer to the previous lesson pages as they work.
2. Have them proof the information they write on their box's faces before taping the finished Talking Box together.

Closing: Ask your students why these might be called *Talking Boxes* and what information the Talking Boxes share. Should all of the Talking Boxes say the same thing? Why or why not? Does the information on all of the students' Talking Boxes match? Have students check their measurements against the answer key.

lesson 5
make a talking box

Materials: ruler, calculator, scissors, tape

1. Look at the box pattern on the Talking Box Pattern handout, but don't cut it out.

   Write your name on the box.

   Write the number of bases on the box.

   Write the number of lateral faces on the box.

   Write the number of right angles inside the box.

   Determine the total surface area of the box and record.

   Compute the volume of the box and record.

2. Cut out the box, fold on the lines, and tape it together. Make sure the information your box shares is on the outside of the box.

   Compare your talking boxes. Do they all say the same thing?

talking box pattern

4"

Number of Right Angles _____

2"

Name _____

Number of Lateral Faces _____

Total Surface Area = _____ sq. in.

Number of Bases _____

Volume = _____ cubic inches

Rectangular Box Pattern: 4" x 2" x 2"

Lesson 6
Reflecting

Grade Level: 4–5

Approximate Length of Time: 15 minutes

Rationale: Students are given the opportunity to identify what has been learned in the Geometry Box Project and think about its application to a new shape.

National Standard Addressed: Students will analyze characteristics and properties of two- and three-dimensional shapes.

Objectives: Students will be able to:
- summarize what they have learned about the attributes of a box, or right rectangular prism,
- explain the use of square units for measuring area and cubic units for measuring volume, and
- apply what they have learned about area and volume of right rectangular prisms as they make a prediction about finding the area and volume of a pyramid.

Materials: No additional materials needed.

Procedure:

Opening: Tell students they will be given time to think about the things they have learned in The Geometry Box Project, write their responses, and share with the group.
Development of Lesson: Have students complete Lesson 6 independently.
Closing/Assessment: Students share responses from items 1–3 on their student worksheet.

Assessment: Evaluate student responses during the lesson's closing. Do student responses show understanding of the terms *base, face, lateral face, parallel faces,* and *right angle*? Do student responses indicate that area is used with two-dimensional figures and volume is used with three-dimensional solids? Do students recognize that to compute total surface area of a pyramid, they would need a method for finding the area of a triangle?

Independent Activities/Lesson Extension/Adaptations:

Allow interested students to browse through references such as *Cliffs Quick Review: Geometry* and examine the formulas for computing the volume of pyramids, cones, and other solids.

lesson 6
reflecting

1. What do you know about right rectangular prisms that you didn't know before the Geometry Box Project?

_____

_____

_____

2. How would you explain to someone why square units are used for area and cubic units are used for volume?

_____

_____

_____

3. Stretch:
How would computing total surface area and volume of a pyramid differ from the methods used for right rectangular prisms?

_____

_____

_____

Share your responses with your group members.

Answer Key for Geometry Box Project

Lesson 1:

1. All angles are right angles. They are three-dimensional.
2. Sides/faces: 6; Sets of parallel faces: 3; Right angles: 24; 3 right angles on each of the 8 corners. Students should use a protractor or a corner of a piece of paper to find the three right angles on each corner.
3. "Base" should be taped to the top and bottom of the box; "lateral face" should be taped to each side of the box.

Lesson 2:

1. The number of square units in a flat figure (students' wording may vary).
2. Answers will vary with boxes used
3a. Answers will vary with boxes used
3b. The area of a face is labeled with square inches because a face is two-dimensional and two-dimensional objects are measured in square inches (units).
4a. Total surface area = the areas of each side of the box added together
4b. By adding the areas of each side of the box together.

Lesson 3:

1. Answers will vary by box
2. The formula works because total surface area is the sum of the areas of the six faces of the box. There are three sets of parallel faces. 2lw is one set of parallel faces, 2lh is another set of parallel sides, and 2wh is the third set. Added together, they give the total surface area.
3. Answers will vary by box

Lesson 4:

1. The amount of space occupied by a three-dimensional object, or the space inside an object. Wording will vary.
2. Volume: Answers will vary with boxes used
3. Analyze: Answers will vary with boxes used
4a. Volume = length x width x height (or V = l x w x h). Volume is three-dimensional, so three measurements are used.
4b. Area/Volume: Area is two-dimensional, so two measurements are used. Volume is three-dimensional, so three measurements are used.

Lesson 5:

Number of bases: 2
Number of lateral faces: 4
Number of right angles: 24
Total surface area for a box 4 in. x 2 in. x 2 in. is 40 square inches
Volume is 16 cubic inches

About the Authors

Diana Goodwin Brigham earned a bachelor's degree in education from Texas Tech University, and a master's degree in education from Arizona State University. She also received a master's degree in gifted education from Hardin-Simmons University in Abilene, TX. Currently, she teaches third grade gifted students in a pull-out program. She has also taught at Hardin-Simmons University as a part-time instructor and has published articles in *Tempo* magazine. Diana has been honored as Teacher of the Year at Austin Elementary and the Region 13 teacher of the year for gifted students in 1998.

Jessica Fell lives and teaches in beautiful British Columbia. After graduating from the University of British Columbia in 2003, she decided to pursue a master's degree in special education, which she will obtain in April 2006. As a learner support teacher for the Surrey School District, she considers all of her students when developing curriculum and differentiates instruction to involve every student in the learning process. Jessica plans to expand her focus to include children's books in the near future.

Constance Simons works as a gifted education facilitator and teacher in a public school program for gifted students. Her role includes working with small groups of mathematically talented fourth and fifth graders. She received her bachelor's degree from Drake University and a master's degree from the University of Nebraska.

Kathy Strunk was born and raised as one of eight children in the small town of Oneida, TN, where she continues to live with her husband, working as a substitute elementary school teacher for the Scott County Board of Education. After many years of working in an office and raising her three children, Kathy wanted to continue working with and teaching children on a professional level. She attended community college by night, and at the age of 45, received her bachelor's and teaching degrees from the University of the Cumberlands. Kathy feels blessed to continue to share her education and experience by creating engaging lessons for her students.

Anthony Yodice has been at Metrolina Regional Scholars' Academy, a public charter school for highly gifted students in Charlotte, NC, since 2001. He received his BA in secondary education and history at the State University of New York at Cortland and his gifted certification from the University of North Carolina at Charlotte. He currently teaches social studies to fifth through eighth graders and continues to improve the social studies curricula he developed for K–8 classrooms.

For Product Safety Concerns and Information please contact our EU
representative GPSR@taylorandfrancis.com Taylor & Francis Verlag GmbH,
Kaufingerstraße 24, 80331 München, Germany

Printed and bound by CPI Group (UK) Ltd, Croydon, CR0 4YY

17/04/2025

01847974-0001